The Story Cycle Method Companion Workbook

Additional Publications by Sascha Brown Rice

The Story Cycle Method: A Practical Playbook for Writers and Dreamers

The Companion Journals:

The Compass Notebook: A Story Cycle Guided Journal

The Field Notes Writing Tracker: A Story Cycle Process Journal

MUSE & MOON
PUBLISHING

The Story Cycle Method Companion Workbook

Writing Prompts and Activities

Sascha Brown Rice

The Story Cycle Companion Workbook:
Writing Prompts and Activities

Copyright © 2023 by Sascha Brown Rice

First Edition
Printed in the United States of America.

ISBN: 979-8-9873195-6-7, paperback
ISBN: 979-8-9873195-7-4, ebook

Book design & typesetting by HR Hegnauer

MUSE & MOON
PUBLISHING

Muse & Moon Publishing
Los Angeles, California
www.museandmoonpublishing.com

This book belongs to

_____

Date: _____

Dear Writer,

Congratulations! You're here!

This workbook is designed to give you space to tackle the exercises in *The Story Cycle Method: A Practical Playbook for Writers and Dreamers.*

Ditch the rules and let go of the idea of "good writing." I give you permission to be imperfect, silly, or even stupid. In fact, I challenge you to do some truly terrible writing here. Your workbook is a safe space for bad ideas.

Before you decide if an idea is any good, you need to get words on the page. Even before you write your shitty first draft, you need to experiment and explore. There'll be time to discard and draft later—but first, let's play.

Let's go!

XO

Table of Contents

Part VI: That's a Wrap

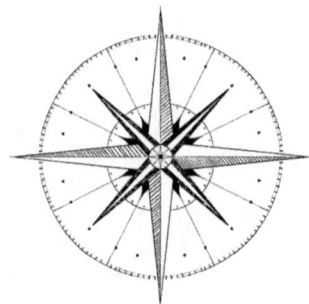

Introduction

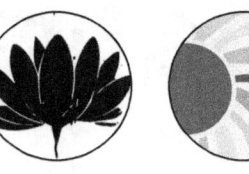

Introduction

This workbook contains the writing prompts and exercises from *The Story Cycle Method: A Practical Playbook for Writers and Dreamers*. Trust the organic ebb and flow of the creative process. This isn't a race. Savor the journey. The workbook is organized into six parts, so you might give yourself two months to work through the exercise. Or you might take a year to work your way through the whole book.

A creative journey rarely follows a neat, linear path and inspiration can feel like the weather, but productivity doesn't need to be ruled by illusive forces.

With the Story Cycle mindset, we can weather the seasons of creativity.

- ◎ Winter is an opportunity to *calibrate:* to listen, reflect, and dream. The *airy* stillness gives us permission to pause and reflect.

- ❧ The spring season is when we *cultivate:* plant and prepare. *Water* invigorates the process of discovery and development.

- ☀ The summer cycle is an invitation to play, improvise, and *collaborate*. In this cycle, *fire* sparks joy and ignites inspiration.

- ▲ The *Craft* Cycle is anchored in autumn: fall heralds the harvest. The *earthy* pragmatics help us revise, refine, and complete.

There's no need to rush. If you're like most people, you have responsibilities. Start by devoting ten minutes a day to your writing.

Tip: If you are juggling a busy schedule, simply start with the time you have.

ACTIVITY: Compass Notebook

Dedicate a journal to tackling the exercises in the book.

- ☐ Any old notebooks will do, but consider using
  The Compass Notebook: A Story Cycle Guided Journal
- ☐ Once you have your notebook, you'll be ready to tackle the exercises in Chapter One.

Purchase:
The Compass Notebook

_____

_____

_____

_____

_____

_____

_____

_____

_____

_____

_____

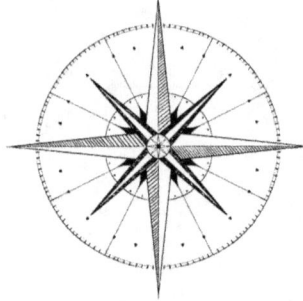

PART I

Calibrate

THE WINTER CYCLE

Chapter One: The Pause
- ☐ Make a Writing Date
- ☐ Choose a Journal
- ☐ Freewrite Prompts

Chapter Two: Radical Self-Care
- ☐ The Body Check-In
- ☐ Count Your Blessings
- ☐ Make a Self-Care Cheat Sheet

Chapter Three: Wonder
- ☐ Right Now
- ☐ Field Notes Writing Tracker
- ☐ Build the Bridge
- ☐ Quick Calibration

Chapter Four: Why
- ☐ Calibrate with Why
- ☐ Story Cycle Survey

Calibrate Your Compass

Snow day: If energy wanes, indulge the urge to hibernate and cocoon.
☐ Spend Sunday morning in bed, make a pot of tea, or cozy up with a book.

The Pause

Winter: It's time to calibrate: to reflect and listen. Settle into stillness.

RECAP: Honor the Pause

The creative process spirals through the Story Cycles, so make it a habit to pause and calibrate. If you feel restless, it may be because you are ready to migrate to the next cycle, or it might just be a case of spring fever. Before you move from winter to spring, consider this quick calibration.

We can invoke the pause by using the foundational tools: the timer and freewriting. No matter what cycle you are moving through, it's important to make time to calibrate.

Tools and Techniques

- ◎ The pause
- ◎ Timer
- ◎ Freewriting

Chapter One Activities

ACTIVITY: Choose a Journal   🕐 30 minutes

If you haven't already, pick a notebook.

- ☐ Designate a notebook specially dedicated to tackling the exercises in the book. Any old notebook will do, but consider using
  The Compass Notebook: A Story Cycle Guided Journal

Purchase:
The Compass Notebook

Make a Writing Date   🕐 10 minutes

- ☐ Look at the next week and assess how much time you have available.
- ☐ Schedule two to five writing sessions in your calendar.
  - The sessions may be anywhere from three minutes to three hours.
  - If you have only one hour in the week to work with, then I recommend starting with three twenty-minute blocks.

Freewrite   🕐 4 minutes

Use freewriting to explore the prompts below. Don't stop writing. Keep the pen moving. Let a stream of consciousness flow on the page. When you get stuck, return to the guiding prompt and rewrite the prompt until a new idea presents itself. You can even write and rewrite "what's next" until a new idea pops up. Keep going. What's next, what's next, what's next, what's next …

Remember: this is a way to warm up, so lower the stakes and have fun. (Dedicate two minutes to each prompt.)

Prompts:
- ☐ *I feel …*
- ☐ *I want …*

CHAPTER TWO

Radical Self-Care

Winter: The Calibrate Cycle reminds us to rest and refill the well.

RECAP: Protect your Practice

Practicing radical self-care helps us protect our writing practice. Without regular self-care, the stresses of everyday life will erode your writing practice. Calibrating with radical self-care helps the writer weather the seasons of creativity. Techniques like the body check-in and the gratitude list are accessible ways to calibrate. These practices provide a reliable way to get centered and give us access to our inner world. We expand our understanding of self-care by tending to the eight realms of radical self-care.

Tools and Techniques

- ◎ The body check-in
- ◎ List making
- ◎ Radical self-care
- ◎ Eight realms

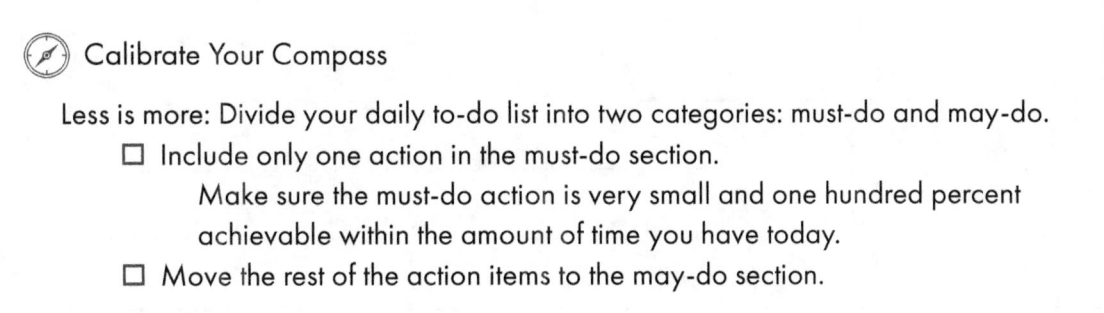

◈ Calibrate Your Compass

Less is more: Divide your daily to-do list into two categories: must-do and may-do.
- ☐ Include only one action in the must-do section.
  Make sure the must-do action is very small and one hundred percent achievable within the amount of time you have today.
- ☐ Move the rest of the action items to the may-do section.

Chapter Two Activities

ACTIVITY: The Body Check-In   ⏰ 3 minutes

No one knows you like you. Tap into your inner world. What do you notice?

- ☐ Settle into a comfortable seated position, then set a timer for two minutes.
- ☐ Close your eyes and observe your breath.
- ☐ Turn your attention inward.
- ☐ Notice the sensations in your body and the chatter in the mind, then come back to your breath.
- ☐ When the timer goes off, open your eyes, pull out your journal, and set the timer for one minute.
- ☐ *Jot down your observations.*
- ☐ *What did you notice?*
- ☐ *What's on your mind? How is your body?*
- ☐ *Do you need to calibrate with self-care?*
- ☐ *Did something come up about your writing project?*

Download:
The Body Check-in Guided Meditation

_____

_____

_____

_____

_____

Count Your Blessings: Make a Gratitude List

⏰ 7 minutes

Make a gratitude list. Try to identify twenty blessings.

☐ Use list making to give thanks.
  - Nothing is too small to be on the list: oxygen, clean drinking water, apples, water, socks.
  - Consider the eight realms.

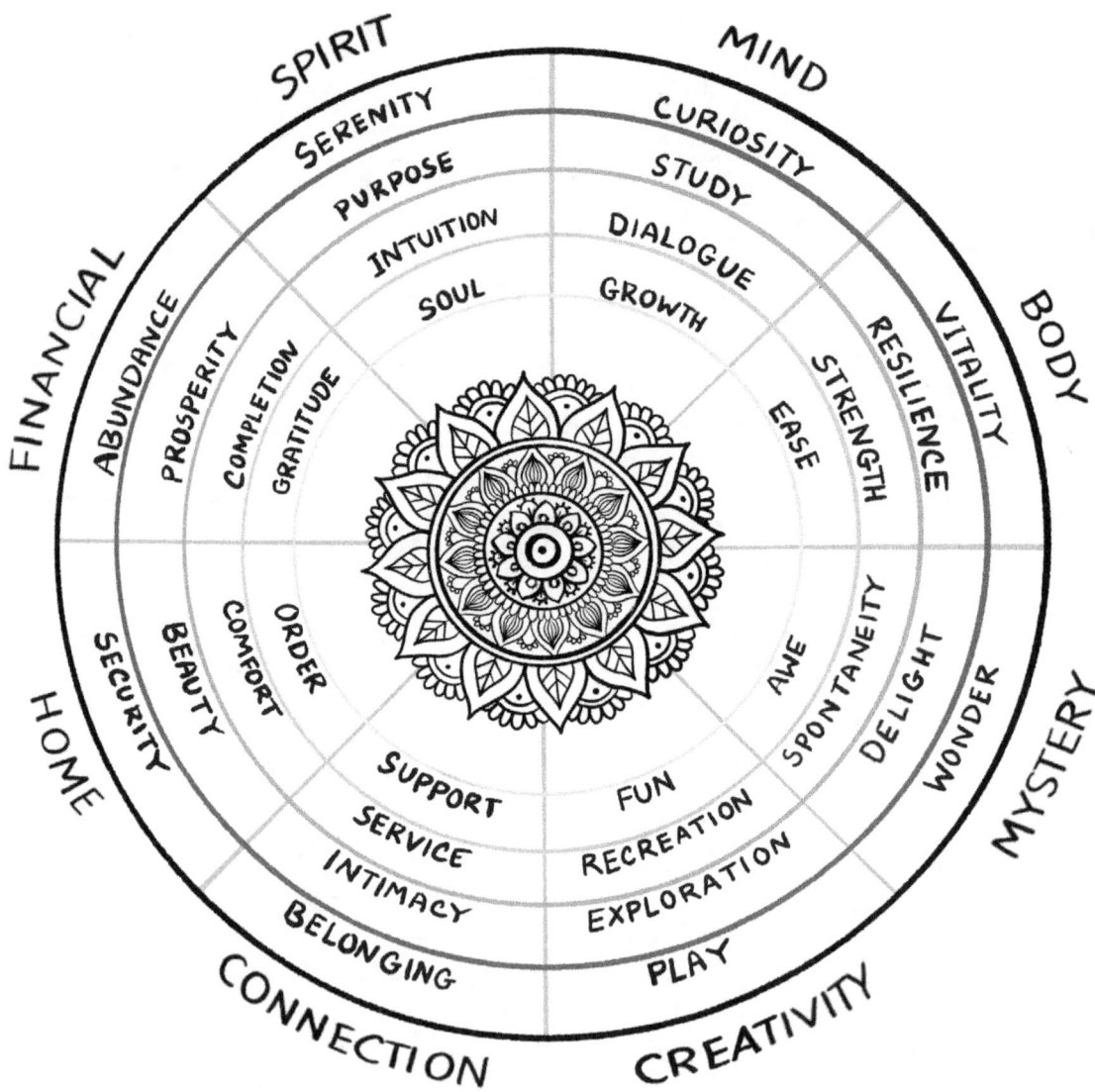

Make a Self-Care Cheat Sheet 🕐 30 minutes

Make a list of actions that support your physical, emotional, social, and spiritual well-being. Look for ways to nourish your body, mind, and spirit. Try this five-step process.

Step 1: Freewrite. 7 minutes
Muse on what radical self-care means to you.
PROMPT: *Radical self-care is . . .*

Step 2: Make a list. 7 minutes
Look over your freewrite, then brainstorm a list of self-care activities. Consider these questions:
- ☐ *What activities and experiences are restorative to me?*
- ☐ *Where do I find spiritual connection and serenity?*
- ☐ *What do I do (or did I do) for fun? (What did I do for fun when I was in elementary school?)*
- ☐ *Where do I find beauty, inspiration, and joy?*
- ☐ *Who are the people who bring me joy and calm?*
- ☐ *How do I like to connect to nature?*
- ☐ *If I had infinite time and money, what would self-care look like for me?*

You can return to this freewrite anytime, but for now, stop after seven minutes.

Step 3: Make your cheat sheet. 10 minutes
Reread your list and make a list of twenty self-care actions. Include a range of actions from teeny-tiny to grandiose.

Step 4: Schedule it! 5 minutes
Select three actions from your cheat sheet and schedule them for some time within the next two weeks.
Tip: Remember to consider the eight realms of self-care.

Step 5: Do it! 1 minute
Select one tiny action from your cheat sheet and do it right now.

Ready to go further?

Make a self-care menu.

Download:
The Self-Care Menu Template

_____

_____

_____

_____

_____

_____

_____

_____

_____

_____

_____

_____

_____

Calibrate Your Compass

Ice Breaker: If you're feeling cabin fever, do something to change up the energy.
☐ Prepare yourself a special beverage, change your scenery, or light a candle.

CHAPTER THREE

Wonder

Winter: To calibrate we connect to curiosity and reclaim wonder.

RECAP: Calibrate and Continue

By adopting the explorer mindset, we renew a sense of wonder. The practice of keeping field notes will help you understand your process. When you pause to calibrate, you can continue forward with more clarity. The simple but powerful ritual of the bridge helps us transition from the everyday into a creative mindset.

Tools and Techniques

- Wonder
- Explorer mindset
- Field notes
- The bridge
- Quick calibration

Chapter Three Activities

Right Now

🕐 7 minutes

Pick a priority. What is the most important priority right now?

- ☐ Make an action list.
    - Brainstorm all the actions you want/need to take.
    - Consult your question list for ideas.
- ☐ Take a moment to calibrate.
    - Where are you in the Story Cycles?
    - What actions match this cycle?
    - What do you need to do before moving into the next cycle?
- ☐ Pick one priority and clearly identify a specific task that relates to that goal.

ACTIVITY: The Field Notes Writing Tracker

Dedicate a specific notebook focused on your process. In addition to your Compass Notebook, where you're freewriting and doing exercises, you'll also want a Field Notes Writing Tracker entirely devoted to charting your writing journey.

- ☐ Designate a journal for tracking and observing your process.
    Any old notebooks will do, but consider using *The Field Notes Writing Tracker.*

 The Field Notes Writing Tracker:
A Story Cycle Process Journal

Build the Bridge

After your next writing session, use the bridge questions to create a path back to the world of your story.

- ☐ *What did I plan to do?*
- ☐ *What did I do?*
- ☐ *What do I need to do next?*
    - Is there an exercise or task you'd like to repeat?
    - Give yourself suggestions on what to do next.

_____

_____

_____

_____

_____

_____

_____

_____

_____

_____

_____

_____

_____

Quick Calibration

In your Field Notes Writing Tracker, take a moment to calibrate. Check in and reflect. How do you feel about your writing today?

- ☐ Jot down observations about the activity.
  - Was the exercise useful?
  - If so, why?
  - If not, why not?
- ☐ What could make your writing session more pleasurable and joyful?
  - Make a physical sensory change to your writing space. For example, pick a flower, brew a cup of tea, pull out that fancy notebook you've been saving, or light a candle.

_____

_____

_____

_____

_____

_____

_____

_____

_____

_____

_____

_____

Calibrate Your Compass

Bird's-eye View: Look at the big picture. Where do you want to be in five years?
☐ Use freewriting to explore.

CHAPTER FOUR

Why

Winter: Shift the focus from external to internal.

RECAP: The Big Picture

Along your writing journey, take time to calibrate your creative compass. Tapping into your *why* helps you stay on track. Consider where you are in the process, connect with your intentions, and zoom out to look at the big picture. As we spiral through the Story Cycles, we can also calibrate with The Story Cycle survey.

Tools and Techniques

- ◎ The why
- ◎ Bird's-eye view
- ◎ The Story Cycle survey

Chapter Four Activities

Calibrate with *Why*

🕑 6 minutes

Open the portal to your process with the magic key: Why?

In your Field Notes Tracker, use freewriting to explore the questions below. (2 minutes each)

- ☐ Why write? Why do you want to tell this story? Why do you care?
- ☐ Why you? Why are you the person to tell this story?
- ☐ Why now? Why does the world need this story now? Why do you need to write this now?

_____

_____

_____

_____

_____

_____

_____

_____

_____

_____

_____

Story Cycle Survey

 30 minutes

The Story Cycle survey is a quick assessment to help you identify where you are in the Story Cycles so you can determine the best course of action. In Part I of the survey, you'll answer five multiple-choice questions. Next, in Part II, use the answer key to calibrate. Finally, in Part III, you'll wrap up with freewriting. Use your Field Notes Writing Tracker to write and reflect. Have fun. There are no wrong answers. Select all answers that apply.

Survey Part I: Reflect and Answer

1. What is your current project?

    A. Memoir

    B. Novel

    C. Script

    D. Essay

    E. No F*cking idea!

2. What is the status of the project?

    A. Seedling of an idea

    B. Sh*tty first draft

    C. Developing a concept

    D. Trying to get fired up

    E. Lost in the middle

    F. Almost Done

3. Talk about your process.

    A. I'm most comfortable dreaming and taking time to reflect.

    B. I'm most comfortable developing and brainstorming ideas.

    C. I'm most comfortable exploring, playing, and experimenting.

    D. I'm most comfortable finishing and sharing my ideas with others.

    E. The writing process is mostly uncomfortable.

    F. I have no f*cking idea.

4. Why do you want to write?

    A. I just like writing for the fun of it.

    B. I want to tell great stories that entertain and captivate audiences.

    C. I have a burning desire to tell a specific story.

    D. I want to understand and/or heal trauma.

    E. I want to make an impact and inspire social or political change.

    F. I want to inspire, uplift, and/or bring joy.

5. What are you hoping to gain by reading this book?

    A. I'd be happy if I were writing a few hours a week.

    B. I would love to feel more confident in my writing.

    C. I'm mostly focused on establishing my writing practice.

    D. I want to crank out a draft and need tools to find a path and build momentum.

    E. I want to take my draft to the next level and need help getting to the finish line.

    F. Something else.

Survey Part II: Calibrate

Here is an answer key with some thoughts to help you interpret your answers from Part I.

1. What is your curent project?

If you already know what type of project you are writing, identify three titles similar to your project (or titles that you want your project to be like!)

If you don't know what you want to write, pick out five books, movies, essays, or shows that you love. (These will come in handy in Chapter Eleven.)

2. What is the status of your project?

Given where you are in the process, what is the next milestone?
- Identify three small measurable markers on the way to that milestone.

* See Chapters Four and Sixteen to learn about milestones and markers.

3. Talk about your process

Given what you know about your process, what Story Cycle is most comfortable for you? Which is most challenging?

- If you selected A, then you like dreaming and taking time to reflect. You likely feel at home in the winter Story Cycle of calibration.

- If you selected B, you like developing and brainstorming ideas. You may find you are most at home in the lively activity of the cultivate phase.

- If you selected C, your sweet spot is goofing around and exploring. So, you likely feel at home in the summery, free-flowing Collaborate Cycle.

- If you selected D, you love finishing and fine-tuning, and you're a fan of the Craft Cycle. If you are desperate to finish, share your work and reap the rewards of the harvest. But if you feel stuck, then don't get too cozy in the Craft Cycle. Shake up your process with activities from the Cultivate or Collaborate Cycles. If you've lost your way, circle back to the Calibrate Cycle.

- If you selected E or F, then the writing process is mostly uncomfortable, or you have no f*cking idea what to do next. No problem! You are in the right place. This book will guide you to clarity and help you build the next steps. For now, focus on noticing which Story Cycles are comfortable and which are uncomfortable for you.

4. Why do you want to write?

- If you selected A, good news: you will find lots of new ways to have fun throughout the book.

- If you selected B, then take extra care to connect with your audience. (Pay special attention to Chapter Thirteen.)

- If you selected C, that's great! The book is full of exercises that will help you move forward. To begin, clarify your why.

- If you selected D, then prioritize radical self-care and get to know your inner critic.

- If you selected E, awesome! The book will offer lots of ways to get your ideas onto the page. Be mindful not to get stuck in the Calibrate Cycle, but also don't rush to the Craft Cycle. Remember to clarify your why.

- If you selected F, you will find helpful exercises in the Collaborate Cycle. While you may think your audience is your anchor, to write with authenticity, you'll want to focus your why. Spend time calibrating and give space for discovery with activities related to cultivating.

5. What are you hoping to gain by reading this book?

   After considering the preceding questions, is your goal realistic? If not, time to calibrate!

Survey Part III: Now write about it.

In your Field Notes Writing Tracker, use freewriting to review and reflect.

- Looking at your results, what do you notice?
- What cycle are you moving through?
- Do your goals match the cycle?
- Is your goal realistic?
- Calibrate.
- What's the next step?

_____

_____

_____

_____

_____

_____

_____

_____

_____

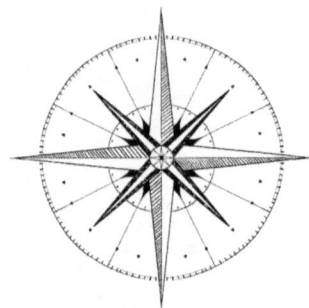

PART II

Cultivate

THE SPRING CYCLE

Chapter Five: Capacity
- ☐ What's my Capacity?
- ☐ Twenty Shades of Gray

Chapter Six: Discovery
- ☐ Take the Pulse
- ☐ Markers and Milestones
- ☐ Track and Treat

Chapter Seven: Explore and Heighten
- ☐ Question List
- ☐ Explore and Heighten
- ☐ The Body Check-In
- ☐ Feelings Cheat Sheets

Chapter Eight: Roots of Desire
- ☐ Calibrate Your Compass
- ☐ Motivate Me
- ☐ Day of Drama

Calibrate Your Compass

When and where: Start your next writing session by looking at when and where you feel most productive and inspired.

☐ Freewrite about when and where you feel creative and alert.

Capacity

Spring: In the Cultivate Cycle, we toil, till, and tend.
Roll up your sleeves, dig in, and get dirty.

RECAP: Assess the Landscape

To navigate the demanding process of development, assess the landscape of your reality. Consider the weather and terrain. What's happening inside and outside? Check in with your capacity. The plans will change and sometimes we'll go off track, so be ready to adjust expectations. Remember to ask *how*, not *if*.

Tools and Techniques

- ◎ Ask how, not if.
- ◎ Capacity
- ◎ Weather and terrain

Chapter Five Activities

What's my capacity?

🕐 10 minutes

In your Field Notes Writing Tracker, assess your capacity.

☐ How many hours per week can you dedicate to your writing practice?
  - Consider the eight realms.
  - Be conservative. It's better to under-promise and over-deliver.
  - A reasonable goal might start with writing for one to four hours per week.

☐ Look at the next two weeks and identify pockets of time.

☐ Add these writing sessions to your calendar.
  - Even if you only plan to write for ten or fifteen minutes, make an appointment and add that to your schedule.

* *Be realistic.* Consider work, family, health, and recreation.
* Give yourself *buffer time and account for transition time.*

The Ten-Minute Rule

Don't give in to the all-or-nothing mentality. Start with the time you have. Even if you can't write every day, it's worthwhile to write regularly. Build your writing practice minute by minute. Ten minutes of writing a day *will* yield results.

- ☐ Start with three minutes and build from there.

- ☐ Look at the next two weeks and identify pockets of time.

  - Warm up (3 minutes)

  - Free-write or write from a prompt (4 minutes)

  - Bridge (3 minutes)

- ☐ Make your writing space inviting.

  - Dash off a note to yourself with a few words of encouragement.

  - Set a flower on your desk.

  - Leave yourself a little treat: a candy, a beverage, or a piece of chocolate.

Twenty Shades of Gray

🕐 30 seconds

Warm up with list making. Give yourself a short window of time and a challenging target. The inner critic usually loves to quantify and compete, so this keeps the critic busy and gets the creative energy moving.

☐ Set a timer for thirty seconds and write.
☐ Make a list of things that are gray.
☐ Aim for at least twenty items on the list.
☐ Ready? GO!

For example, if the prompt was red, your list might include apple, fire truck, tongue, lipstick, red, red, red, red face, hand, tomato, shoes, red, red, red, anger, ball, balloon, etc.

* *In the spirit of freewriting, if you can't think of something, you may write the prompt until a new idea surfaces. Keep the pen moving!*

Ready to go further?

You can modify this warm-up by using other colors. You may also try it with specific senses. For example, make a list of sounds and focus it with specificity, like "soft" or "loud."

CHAPTER SIX

Discovery

Spring: Honor the gestation phase.
Embrace this delicious time of possibilities.

RECAP: Word by Word

A story is built word by word, sentence by sentence, and scene by scene. The Cultivate Cycle is a fertile time ripe with possibilities, so to move through the spring cycle, set markers and milestones. Discovery writing turns daydreaming into action. Plot the course forward and celebrate along the way.

Tools and Techniques

- Ebb and flow
- Discovery writing
- Measurable markers and milestones
- Celebrate: track and treat

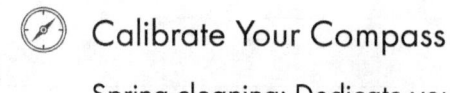 Calibrate Your Compass

Spring cleaning: Dedicate your next writing sessions to getting organized.
- ☐ Clear away the clutter and clean up your action list.

Chapter Six Activities

Take the Pulse

🕐 15 minutes

Look within. Use freewriting to consider where you are.

- ☐ Consider the eight realms.
  - Do you feel full or empty? Energized or exhausted? Isolated or supported?
  - Do you feel connected to your purpose? Curious or confused?
  - How is your body? Do you feel strength and ease?
  - Do you feel safe and secure? Do you feel order and calm?

- ☐ Read and review.
  - Read through your writing. What do you notice?

- ☐ Tend the garden.
  - Make an adjustment to support self-care.

_____

_____

_____

_____

_____

_____

_____

_____

_____

_____

Markers and Milestones

The road to a finished project can be long. Make the process more tangible by identifying manageable and meaningful milestones. Use your Field Notes Writing Tracker or a journal of your choice.

1. Use freewriting to calibrate: clarify where you are starting and where you want to land.

    Set a timer for two minutes and consider these questions:

    > Where are you in your process?
    > What is the ultimate goal?
    > What do you know for sure about your project?

2. Next, use list making to find the concrete steps to move forward on your path.

    Set a timer for four minutes and make a list of all the pieces of the puzzle.

    For example, identify the various elements you want to develop:

    - key events
    - characters
    - important details about setting
    - topics to research
    - books/movies to watch for inspiration
    - outline

3. Pick ONE action to start your next session with.

Reminder: Calibrate after each exercise with a mini bridge.
Jot down observations about the activity.

> Was the exercise useful?
> If so, why?
> If not, why not?

Track and Treat

 20+ minutes

Take your process to the next level and plan how you will celebrate the milestone once you've reached that goal.

Step 1: What upcoming transition or milestone might you mark?

☐ In your Field Notes Writing Tracker, use freewriting to identify possible milestones on your writing journey and important transitions.

Step 2: How do you like to celebrate? What fuels your muse?

☐ Use freewriting to reflect on how you like to celebrate wins.
Here are examples of ways to celebrate:
- Gathering with others
- Treats and rewards
- Scenic view
- Historical marker
- Rest stop
- Refueling

Step 3: What type of treats do you prefer?

☐ Use freewriting to get specific.
- Do you enjoy consumables like food, drinks, or experiences?
- Do you prefer gathering treasures from nature?
- Do you like adding art objects to your writing space?
- Do you like buying yourself jewelry or other wearables like clothing, shoes, or accessories?
- Do you like buying statuettes or icons of spiritual deities to set on your desk?

Tip: Look at your self-care cheat sheet for ideas.

Step 4: Pick a milestone to mark and match with a celebration.

☐ Review your freewrite and plan a celebration.

Step 5: Celebrate!

☐ Do it!

 Download
The Treat Tracker

Explore and Heighten

Spring: The Cultivate Cycle is a time of daring. Embrace the mystery.

RECAP: Move into the Mystery

The development process is all about moving into the mystery. The writer can liberate themselves from the comfort and safety of the known by employing the "Yes, and" technique. Spring is a time to explore and heighten. The writer nourishes their story by digging into the muck: in other words, emotions and senses. It's easy to get distracted during the Cultivate Cycle, so instead of getting stuck in whirlpools of wonder, set questions aside on your question list.

Tools and Techniques

- ◎ Yes, and . . .
- ◎ Explore and heighten
- ◎ Emotions and senses (the muck)
- ◎ The question list

⊚ **Calibrate Your Compass**

Spring in Your Step: It's easy to get stuck in the development process. To move through the muck, move your body.
- ☐ Get your heart pumping, stretch, or simply go barefoot.

Chapter Seven Activities

Question List

⏰ 5 minutes

There are no dumb questions, but there are distracting ones. Free up your mental bandwidth and make a question list. Rather than wondering or worrying about how, who, what, when, why, and where, write the question down. Use freewriting and list making to generate questions.

- ☐ First, identify the focus of the question list.
  - It may center around a specific project you are working on, an idea that you are exploring, or it might relate to process.
- ☐ Next, write all the questions floating around in your head.
  (Include anything that you are pondering.)
  - For example, consider decisions that you need to make, events that you are contemplating, characters who are unformed, outcome options, possibilities, etc.
  - Challenge yourself to identify twenty questions.

Tip: Keep your question list in a place that's easy to find. I recommend dedicating a special page in your Field Notes Writing Tracker.

_____

_____

_____

_____

_____

_____

_____

_____

Explore and Heighten

Write about a mundane event with intense detail. Transport your reader by bringing the senses alive. Consider your vantage point. You may choose to:

- Write from the point of view of one of your characters.
- Write from your point of view and state of mind today.
- Explore the emotions of an ordinary moment in your story (especially for memoir writers).

Step 1. Put your character in a no or low-stakes situation. The more boring the better.   1 minute

☐ Here are examples of no/low-stakes events:

- eating breakfast
- brushing teeth
- tying shoes
- making the bed
- walking into the kitchen
- opening a door
- flushing a toilet

Step 2. Pick an emotion to explore and heighten.   1 minute

☐ Select the core emotion you want to explore.

- Happy, loving, sad, angry, or fearful

Refer to the Feelings Cheatsheets on pages 58-59.

Step 3. Next, select an even more specific version of that emotion.   1 minute

- Look at the feelings list for ideas.

Step 4. Use freewriting to describe the minutiae of the scene.   5 minutes

- Explore and heighten the emotions.

Step 5. Review your writing and record your observations.   2 minutes

- Jot down your observations in your journal.
- What did you discover about your character?
- Add questions to the question list.
- Make notes about your process in your Field Notes Writing Tracker.

_____

_____

_____

_____

_____

_____

_____

_____

_____

_____

_____

_____

_____

_____

_____

_____

_____

_____

_____

FEELINGS CHEATSHEET
Feelings When Needs Are Met

HAPPY

Adventurous
Amazed
Amused
Astonished
Curious
Delighted
Determined
Eager
Ecstatic
Encouraged
Excited
Fascinated
Giddy
Hopeful

Inspired
Intrigued
Invigorated
Joyful
Overjoyed
Refreshed
Relieved
Stimulated
Surprised
Thrilled
Touched
Trusting
Upbeat

CONTENT

Alive
Confident
Glad
Grateful
Peaceful
Pleased
Relaxed
Satisfied
Tranquil

LOVING

Affectionate
Friendly
Moved
Proud
Thankful

FEELINGS CHEATSHEET
Feelings When Needs Are Not Met

FEARFUL

Afraid
Alarmed
Anxious
Apprehensive
Bewildered
Cautious
Concerned
Confused
Disconcerted
Disturbed
Dubious
Embarrassed
Impatient

Jittery
Nervous
Overwhelmed
Panicky
Perplexed
Puzzled
Reluctant
Restless
Scared
Shocked
Stressed
Terrified
Worried

ANGRY

Aggravated
Agitated
Annoyed
Apart
Cranky
Disgusted
Exasperated
Frustrated
Furious
Impatient
Indignant
Infuriated
Irritated
Resentful
Upset

SAD

Bored
Depressed
Disappointed
Discouraged
Disheartened
Dismayed
Grieving
Helpless
Hopeless
Hurt
Lonely
Melancholic
Tired
Troubled

FAUX FEELINGS

Abandoned	Ignored	Neglected
Abused	Intimidated	Put Upon
Attacked	Invisible	Rejected
Betrayed	Let Down	Rushed
Bullied	Manipulated	Unappreciated

_____
_____
_____
_____
_____
_____
_____
_____
_____
_____
_____
_____

Ready to go further?

Try out one of these options:

- Continue to explore that emotion with freewriting.
- Explore the same emotion from a different character's point of view.
- For nonfiction writers, use freewriting to write about a key moment when this emotion is in play.

 Download
The Feelings Cheat Sheet

_____

_____

_____

_____

_____

_____

_____

_____

_____

_____

CHAPTER EIGHT

Roots of Desire

Spring: It's time to cultivate. When we plant, we must fortify the soil.

RECAP: Raise the Stakes

When your writing feels flat or dull, it's time to cultivate. If your character is sailing along without a care in the world, it's time to excavate obstacles using the tools and techniques of the spring cycle. By developing desires, secrets, and fears, we discover how to complicate the character's journey. Knowing a character's fears gives new ways to create consequences that amp up the tension and raise the stakes. What are they willing to do to protect a secret? When you want to pour Miracle-Gro on your story, dive into drama and make trouble.

Tools and Techniques

- ◎ Make trouble
- ◎ Desire and motivation
- ◎ Secrets and fears

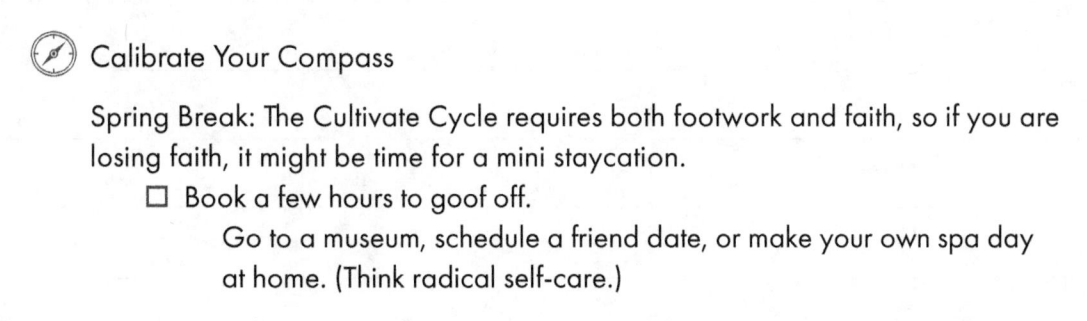

🧭 Calibrate Your Compass

Spring Break: The Cultivate Cycle requires both footwork and faith, so if you are losing faith, it might be time for a mini staycation.
- ☐ Book a few hours to goof off.
     Go to a museum, schedule a friend date, or make your own spa day at home. (Think radical self-care.)

Chapter Eight Activities

Calibrate Your Compass

⏰ 7 minutes

In your Field Notes Writing Tracker, take a moment to calibrate your creative compass.

🧭 Check in and reflect on your current progress and the process.

- ☐ Use freewriting to explore these questions:
  - *How do I feel about the process?*
  - *What are the obstacles in my way?*
  - *Am I trying to tackle too much at once?*
  - *Does my approach match the story cycle I am moving through?*
  - *Am I clinging to an idea that's no longer relevant?*
- ☐ Read and reflect.
  - *What's the next action?*
  - *Are there small actions I can take?*
  - *Do I need rest?*
  - *Can I make the writing process more pleasurable and joyful?*
- ☐ Calibrate.
  - *Make a physical sensory change to your writing space. For example, pick a flower, brew a cup of tea, pull out that fancy notebook you've been saving, or light a candle.*

_____

_____

_____

_____

_____

RESET: Five Quick Calibrations to Get Back on Track

These five quick calibrations will get you back into the writing groove.
1. Match the approach with the Story Cycle.
2. Focus on the next right action.
3. Do less.
4. Do one thing at a time.
5. Take a mini break.

_____

_____

_____

_____

_____

_____

_____

_____

_____

_____

Motivate Me

Find what's motivating your character. By digging into desire, fear, and secrets, we'll nourish the roots of your story.

Step 1. Warm-Up: I want, I fear

Before we dive into your character's desires, take a moment to personally connect to the energy of desire and fear.

☐ Use freewriting to explore.

   Give yourself three minutes for each prompt.
   - *I want . . .*
   - *I fear . . .*

☐ Jot down insights, observations, questions, or discoveries in your Field Notes Writing Tracker.

   - What did you learn about your process?

Step 2. What's at Stake?

Explore motivation.

☐ Write about what's at stake. Consider these questions:

   - What is motivating your character to keep this secret?
   - Why is this character determined to keep this secret?
   - How does this secret create complications for our character?
   - How might the discovery of this secret make the journey to their goal more difficult?
   - How does this secret raise the stakes?
   - How does the secret align with the character's beliefs and morals?
   - Is this secret relatable?

Step 3. Synthesize

Read over your writing and make note of any insights, takeaways, or questions.

☐ Distill your character's desire using this template.

- The character wants _____
- The main obstacles in the way are_____
- The character's biggest fears are_____
- If the character gets what they want, the payoff will be_____

_____

_____

_____

_____

_____

_____

_____

_____

_____

_____

_____

_____

_____

Day of Drama

Let's make trouble for our character.

Step 1: Make a quick sketch of your body. (2 minutes)

☐ Draw a simple stick figure or crude outline of your body.

Step 2: Label aches and pains. (5 minutes)

☐ Mark up the figure to identify injuries or pains.

- Like list making, the goal is to just jot down a few words. It doesn't need to make sense to anyone but you.
- Identify scars, injuries, deformities, illnesses, bumps, bruises, bites, or breaks.

Step 3: Write about it. Set a timer for five minutes.

☐ Using freewriting, select option A or B and describe in detail a day of drama!

OPTION A: Pick one of your pains and write about that.

OPTION B: Using your pain for inspiration, give your character an injury and write about it.

If you get stuck or want more guidance, consider these questions:

- What happened?
- Where were you (or your character)? Why were you there?
- What time of day was it? What time of year was it? Your age?
- Who was with you? What was the weather like?
- What happened? What happened next?
- Whom did you tell?
- What did people say? What did your partner/parents/boss say?
- What did you feel?
- If your pain were a color, what color would it be?
- Did you ask for help? What were you thinking?!?!
- What hurt the most? What was the scariest part?

TIP: Use the senses.

Ready to go further?

Pick a pain and describe how that created fear or a secret.

 Download
13 Ways to Make Trouble

_____

_____

_____

_____

_____

_____

_____

_____

_____

_____

_____

_____

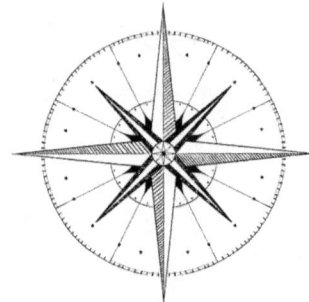

PART III

Collaborate

THE SUMMER CYCLE

Chapter Nine: The Power of Play
- ☐ The Refuge of Storytelling
- ☐ Explore with Word Clouds
- ☐ Dada Daring
- ☐ Tarot or Tea

Chapter Ten: Muse and Critic
- ☐ The Body Check-In
- ☐ Capture the Critic
- ☐ Help Wanted

Chapter Eleven: Facing Feedback
- ☐ Call in your Muse
- ☐ Fan Club
- ☐ Write a Love List

Chapter Twelve: Story RX
- ☐ Story RX
- ☐ Let it Go

The Power of Play

Summer: Shake up the routine, improvise, and play.
It's time to collaborate. Let go of control.

RECAP: Collaborate with Chaos

In this chapter, we use play to tap into our instinctive ability to create stories. The summer cycle is an invitation to wander. It's time to collaborate with the chaos of the world. Nonlinear techniques, like making word clouds and working with tarot, give us access to our unconscious. There's value in going off track. Sometimes there is a breakdown before there is a breakthrough. Sometimes the only way to move forward is to let go of control. With whimsy and serendipity, surrender to the adventure of the summer cycle.

Tools and Techniques

- ◎ Play
- ◎ Collage
- ◎ Word cloud
- ◎ Tarot and tea
- ◎ Wander

🧭 **Calibrate Your Compass**

Summer Daze: When the Collaborate Cycle melts your brain, it's time for some summer fun. A doodle a day keeps the doctor away.
- ☐ Pick a word and start doodling.

Chapter Nine Activities

ACTIVITY: The Refuge of Storytelling

⏰ 7 minutes

In your Field Notes Writing Tracker, use freewriting to explore why you love stories.

☐ Consider these questions:
- What's the first memory you have of writing?
- What's the first story that you remember writing?
- What's the most fun you've had with writing?
- How does it feel to share your writing with others?

Download:
Ignite Inspiration: Five Ways to Get Fired Up

Explore with Word Clouds

⏰ 10 minutes

Create branches to link ideas and build clusters of connections. You may find an unusual discovery that illuminates something you hadn't been able to articulate.

Step 1: Pick a topic.   2 minutes

Step 2: Explore the topic using the word cloud technique.   5 minutes

Step 3: Use the word cloud to freewrite on a topic of your choice.   3 minutes

Examples of topics:

- Fear, Secret
- Lessons, Advice
- amily, Me
- Yesterday, Today, Tomorrow
- Maybe, Yes, No

- All You Need Is Love
- Likes, Dislikes
- I'm Tired Of . . .
- In My Wildest Dreams, I . . .

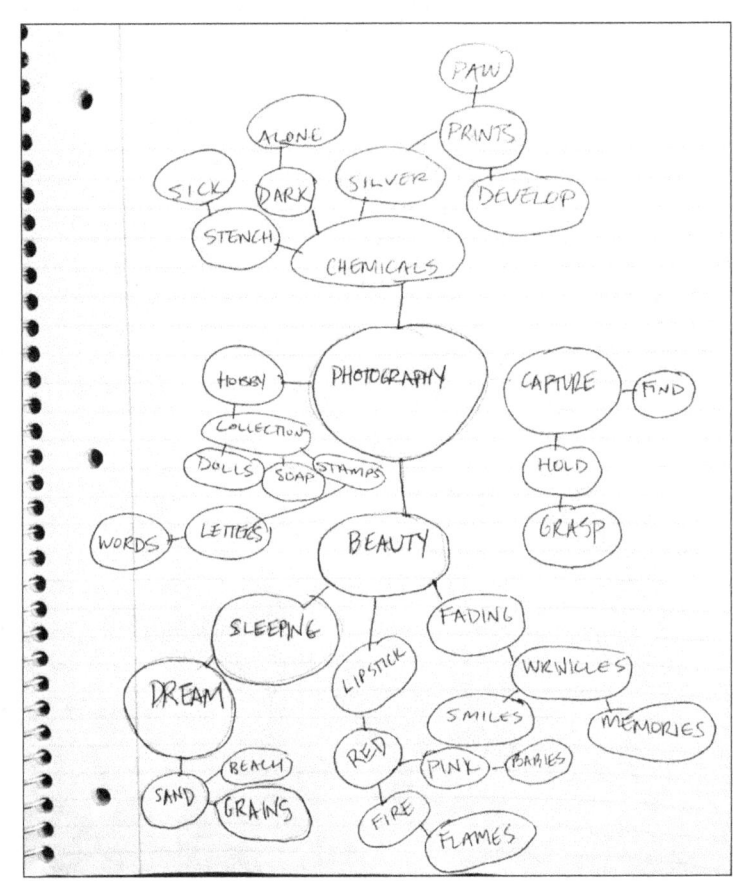

_____

_____

_____

_____

_____

_____

_____

_____

_____

_____

_____

_____

_____

Ready to go further?

Consider using a guiding theme
for branches of the word cloud.
For example, you might use the
senses to spark sensory detail.

Download
3 Word Cloud Templates

Dada Daring

 5–30 minutes

Drawing on the Dadaist sensibility, pull words at random from the Dada Daring Word Bank and let your unconscious guide your writing.

Step 1: Pick three words from the Dada Daring Word Bank on the next page.

Step 2: Write the words in your journal.

Step 3: Freewrite using those words.

 Download
Dada Daring Word Bank

_____

_____

_____

_____

_____

_____

_____

_____

_____

_____

_____

Dada Daring Word Bank

BAREFOOT GLOOM LOST AND FOUND HEAT ACCIDENT MEMORY
LETTER TROUBLED WATERS CONFIDENTIAL PARANORMAL CHASE
HIDE PURSUE ROADBLOCK LOVE   COMPLAINT   UNPLUGGED
EXPECTATION   LOVABLE MONSTER BRAVE WISE BEAUTIFUL
STRONG COLD CRUEL OBEDIENT GIFT BOSSY SCARY GROUCHY
BITTER SELFISH VAIN WARRIOR WARDROBE RAGS BIKINI ARMOR
GOWN WINGS ERUPTION AVALANCHE TSUNAMI BLIZZARD FLOOD
FIRE TORNADO FAMINE LIGHTNING STORM   FOREST WATER
UNDERGROUND DESERT SWAMP FARM COUNTRYSIDE OUTERSPACE
CLOUD CITY FLAG MAP PARALLEL UNIVERSE FOREIGNERS TRAP
DOOR HIDDEN STAIRCASES IMPOSSIBLE ALIBI PROOF MOTIVE
CLUE POSTCARD WILL VOICES GRAVITY SUNRISE SUNSET DUSK
DAWN GROWL HOWL BARK HISS REPAIR RUPTURE VEGETABLE
ABSORB FLOAT FLY FREEZE GLIDE TRASH TREASURE GRACE
METAL WOOD FIREWATER AIR EARTHNOW PRESENT PAST PUBLIC
FUTURE JOKERKING QUEEN JACK   CROOK   POLITICIAN
ENGINEER   CRASH SMASH KISS BIG RAIN LAVA ROCK STAR
SIDEKICK TAROT MONDAY TEEN TODDLER BABY ADULT TWEEN
BROTHER SISTER MOTHER FATHER GRANDPARENT ELDER
BABYSITTER HERO JOURNEYELIXIR CAVE CLIFF MESSAGE SHOW
HIDE   LOSER MOON STARS DICTATOR SON CAPTAIN DROPOUT
SHERIFF HAT GLOVE SOCK SHOE PIANO   DESSERT DINNER
BREAKFAST LUNCH ILLUSION REALITY BODY HOT COLD TIGHT
FACT BURGER FAN DETECTIVE HISTORICAL FIGURE SEASONS
WOLF OWLCAT HOME SUMMER SPRING FALL WINTER HOLIDAY

Tarot or Tea

20 minutes

Option A: Tarot

☐ Pull a tarot card for each question, then pay attention to your gut reaction.

☐ What do the images on the card make you feel? What thoughts pop into your mind?

☐ Jot down your observations.

Note: Most tarot decks come with a "little white book" that explains the traditional meaning of each card, so these details can add another dimension. But, most importantly, tune into what the image sparks inside you.

Download
3 Easy Tarot Story Spreads

_____

_____

_____

_____

_____

_____

_____

_____

_____

_____

Option B: Teatime

Allergic to tarot? It's okay—tarot isn't for everyone. Instead, invite your character over for a chat.

☐ Have a dialogue with your character while you enjoy a cup of tea or a snack.

☐ Write each question in your journal.

☐ Then switch pens and answer.

Questions:

- What do you believe you need to be happy (or loved or fulfilled or accepted or successful)?

- What's your view of the world and your place in it?

- What rules (or restrictions) are pressing on you?

- Are there cultural norms, taboos, or expectations that impact you?

☐ Now read over your writing. What do you notice?

- Record your observations in your Field Notes Writing Tracker.

☐ When you are done, do a little pampering. It's time for a little radical self-care.

- Remember to consider the eight realms.

Tips:

- Characters don't always answer truthfully and may go off on tangents.

- Allow them to rant.

- Listen for false beliefs.

- Are they uninformed or misinformed about how the world works?

- Do they have an incorrect belief about themselves or the world?

_____

_____

_____

CHAPTER TEN

Muse and Critic

Summer: The Collaborate Cycle stirs up fiery energy.
Ignite inspiration: Call in your muse and make friends with your critic.

RECAP: Muse and Critic

Sometimes summer's fiery energy sparks chaos and wakes up the critic. Instead of trying to silence or ignore the critic, make friends and collaborate. Invite your muse to join you on the writing journey. Temper the creative fire by making time to reflect and rejuvenate.

Tools and Techniques

- The critic
- The muse
- Letter writing
- Your ideal reader

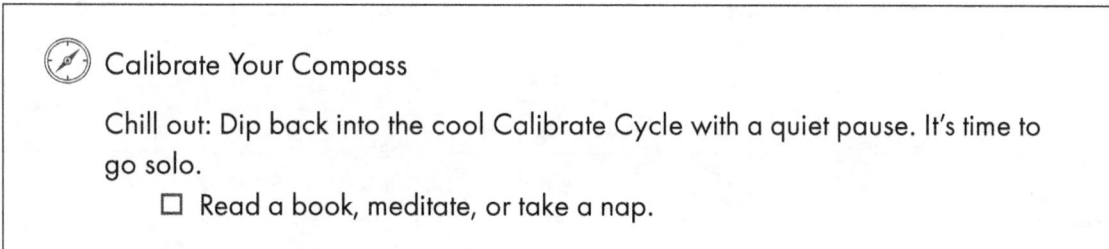

Calibrate Your Compass

Chill out: Dip back into the cool Calibrate Cycle with a quiet pause. It's time to go solo.
- ☐ Read a book, meditate, or take a nap.

Chapter Ten Activities

The Body Check-In

🕐 3 minutes

Do a quick scan. How do I feel in my body?

- ☐ Settle into a comfortable seated position, then set a timer for two minutes.
- ☐ Close your eyes and observe your breath.
- ☐ Turn your attention inward.
- ☐ Notice the sensations in your body, the chatter in the mind, and come back to your breath.
- ☐ When the timer goes off, open your eyes, pull out your journal, and set the timer for one minute.
- ☐ Jot down your observations.
- ☐ *Am I hungry, thirsty, physically off balance?*
- ☐ *Am I feeling lonely or in pain?*
- ☐ *Am I feeling tired or rested?*
- ☐ *Calibrate with self-care.*
- ☐ *Is there something I can do to feel better?*

_____

_____

_____

_____

_____

_____

_____

_____

Capture the Critic

 50 minutes

Let's cozy up to the critic. Let's see their warts and fangs, and we'll listen to their complaints. Next, we'll name them, then finally, we'll write them a love letter.

Step 1: Prepare

5 minutes

☐ Pick your poison.

- You might be wondering how the heck to corral the critic. The simplest approach to tracking your imaginary frenemy is to write in your journal in a question-and-answer format OR you may choose to simply write the critic a letter. (Another option is to do a voice recording and then transcribe it.)

Tip: Use a special color for the critic, so you know these are the critic's words. (Does your critic have a signature color?)

☐ Gather your supplies.

- Your Field Notes Writing Tracker is the perfect place to write down your observations.
- Time and place.
- Assess your state of mind. Is now the right time?
- You will need to be well rested, nourished, and have a clear head.
- Going toe to toe with your critic requires strength. Consider your ability to process information.
- If you are in crisis or exhausted, it is not the right time.
- Schedule it and give them fair warning.

Tip: Avoid spontaneity. Usually, the critic hates surprises.

☐ Set the Mood.

- Create a pleasant experience with candles, soothing music, or a yummy beverage. Be someplace where you feel free to experience emotions.

☐ Begin with a body check-in.

_____

_____

_____

_____

Step 2: Describe your critic in detail.   10 minutes

Consider these questions.

☐ What are your critic's concerns?

- What is worrying them?
- What are they afraid might happen?
- What do they value? What do they fear?
- Write down any messages they have for you.
- What emotions are most alive in this creature?

☐ What do they look and sound like?

- Are they all human or part creature?
- Do they have defining characteristics? Such as fangs, talons, horns, or a tail?
- What do they wear?
- What does their voice sound like? What's their catchphrase?

☐ What's their routine?

- How and where do they spend their days and nights?
- What is their habitat?
- When do they show up?
- Are they a night owl or an early bird?
  Tip: Usually, they are the opposite of what you are.
- What gives them energy? What do they hunt?
- How can they be satisfied? Distracted? Appeased?

☐ What are their special skills? Magical qualities? Graduate degrees?

☐ Does your critic remind you of anyone?

☐ What's your critic's tell?

- Like even the best poker player, your critic has something that will tip you off when they're bluffing. What's their tell?

_____

_____

_____

_____

Step 3: Review and reflect.   7 minutes

☐ Read what you've written.

- What patterns and themes do you notice?
- What topics interest them?
- What insecurities or fears have they tapped?
- Is there a rant running on repeat?
- Have they recycled a story from your past?

Step 4: Give the critic a name.   3 minutes

☐ If a name doesn't spring to mind, give them a nickname.

- The name can be silly or serious.
- We are building a relationship, so be kind.
- Examples: cutie pie, silly goose, tiger

Step 5: Write a love letter to the critic. Consider these topics.   7 minutes

☐ Thank them for looking out for you.

☐ Let them know you will set aside time to listen to their concerns.

☐ Affirm what you love about them. It's important to acknowledge their special talents.

☐ Create a boundary. Request they zip it until their presence is requested.

☐ Thank them again for their ideas and let them know you do not accept unsolicited complaints, critiques, and suggestions.

☐ Reassure them you will be available later.

_____

_____

_____

_____

_____

_____

Step 6: Share your observations with a trusted friend or mentor.   13 minutes

While the exercise outlined is a one-on-one operation, ideally this shouldn't be a solo expedition.

- ☐ Dream Team
  - Who has your back? Involve your muse in this process and assemble a dream team. Build in some extra support with a friend or mentor. Human connection helps you get out of your head.
  - Check in with your original intention.
  - Even with careful planning, you may not achieve the outcome you desire.

Step 7: Bookend with radical self-care.   10 minutes

- ☐ Order up a refill of Story RX or take yourself on an artist date.
  - Consider the eight realms.

Tip: Give the critic an assignment. Help them focus their discerning eyes. Enlist their expertise. Put them to work.

_____

_____

_____

_____

_____

_____

_____

_____

_____

_____

Help Wanted

Prompt: Create a job description for your muse.

Enlist your muse in the project of preparing to put your work into the world.

Step 1: Explore with word clouds.   5 minutes

☐ Identify the qualities you're looking for in your muse.

Step 2: Synthesize your ideas and create a want ad.   5 minutes

☐ Include

- Job title
- Describe position
- Elaborate on job requirements
- Highlight preferred qualities

Step 3: Read and reflect.   5 minutes

Review your writing.

☐ Record observations in your Field Notes Writing Tracker.

Step: 4: Find an image to represent your muse.   5 minutes

☐ Post a picture of your muse where you write.

Step 5: Dedicate a page to your muse.   5 minutes

Onboard your muse.

☐ Welcome the muse to the team.

☐ Reiterate their duties.

☐ Find a picture of your muse to add to your writing desk or paste it into your journal.

CHAPTER ELEVEN

Facing Feedback

*Summer: When the sun burns bright, it's natural to look
for a shady retreat, but when it's time to collaborate,
there's no more hiding, no more secrets.*

RECAP: Facing Feedback

Sharing your writing is an important part of the process, but putting work into the world can be scary. Criticism is valuable, but it can be hard to decipher notes. So, fire up the Collaborate Cycle with the love list and the kind critic. Practicing the art of listening will help you unearth authentic responses during critiques. Calibrating with *why* helps you face feedback by reconnecting to your intention.

Tools and Techniques

- ◎ Facing feedback
- ◎ The art of listening
- ◎ The love list
- ◎ The kind critic

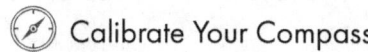 Calibrate Your Compass

Time is on your side: Imagine you have all the time in the world. What would your day look like?
☐ Put something fun on your action list.

Chapter Eleven Activities

Call in your muse.

⏰ 25 minutes

- ☐ Write a note to your muse and invite them to join your next writing session.
- ☐ Make an offering: Light a candle or give them a token of your appreciation: a flower, a piece of fruit, a feather, or a prayer.

_____

_____

_____

_____

_____

_____

_____

_____

_____

_____

_____

_____

_____

_____

Fan Club

Before seeking feedback, reclaim your sense of wonder.

- ☐ Use freewriting to explore.

    Prompt: Wow, you created that!

- ☐ Consider these questions:

    What would the president of your fan club say?

    What hurdles have you overcome?

    Detail your discoveries and victories.

    What do you love about your story?

- ☐ Review and reflect.

    Review your writing and pick out five affirming compliments.

- ☐ Write those affirmations in your Field Notes Writing Tracker.

_____

_____

_____

_____

_____

_____

_____

_____

_____

_____

Write a Love List

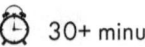

Find at least twenty ways you love your project. Remember, for this exercise, no detail is too small. Search for the aspects to appreciate.

Step 1. Take time to notice what you love and identify specific details.

For example, consider the following:

- ☐ The process
- ☐ The characters
- ☐ Character detail or trait
- ☐ Authentic dialogue
- ☐ A particular line of dialogue
- ☐ A specific moment
- ☐ The period of the story
- ☐ The world of the story
- ☐ Emotional moment [sad, scary, funny]
- ☐ The tone or mood

- ☐ Theme
- ☐ Character name
- ☐ Tension
- ☐ Vivid description
- ☐ Smooth transition
- ☐ The entry point of a scene
- ☐ A resolution
- ☐ Intriguing secret or mystery
- ☐ The intention behind the project
- ☐ Compelling element

Challenge yourself to find at least one thing you love on every page of your piece.

Step 2. Review and reflect.

Read over your love list and record observations in your journal.

Step 3. Highlight.

Select three highlights about your process and add those to your journal.

_____

_____

_____

_____

CHAPTER TWELVE

Story RX

Summer: It's time to stop and smell the flowers. Behold the bloom.

RECAP: Make Peace with the Process

Stop to smell the flowers and enjoy the expansive collaborate cycle. When the summer cycle gets too hot, take time to refill your cup. Even the most carefully nurtured seeds may not sprout. Learn when to hold on and when to let go.

Tools and Techniques

- ◎ Story RX
- ◎ Holding on and letting Go
- ◎ Overwriters and underwriters

◈ Calibrate Your Compass

Summer fling: Put the writing to the side and dabble in another medium.
☐ Pick up a paintbrush, bake a cake, or doodle all day.

Chapter Twelve Activities

ACTIVITY: Story RX   🕐 30+ minutes

It's time to refill your prescription. Make time for a little Story RX.

Step 1. Consult the Story RX and select a treatment.   20 minutes

- ☐ Review the doctor's note and consider which therapy is needed.
  - Media meditation
  - Sound bath
  - Terra therapy
  - Art therapy
  - Lotions and potions
- ☐ Book a fifteen-minute therapy session.
- ☐ Time to dose!

Step 2. Review and reflect.   5 minutes

- ☐ After a dose of Story RX, write about the experience in your Field Notes Writing Tracker.
  - Any new story discoveries or ideas?
  - Any insights into the process?
  - How did it feel?

Step 3. Book a follow-up.

- ☐ Review your writing and schedule your next Story RX session. *Repeat as necessary.*

Download
Story RX

Sascha Brown Rice, S.D.
Story Doctor
Muse & Moon
911 Inspiration Road, Writingtown, CA

Story RX

Date: _____

Take at least one:

- ☐ Media Meditation
- ☐ Sound Bath
- ☐ Terra Therapy
- ☐ Art Therapy
- ☐ Lotions & Potions

DOSE: Take daily or as needed. For best results, combine.
If unable to tolerate the recommended dose, try micro-dosing.

If condition worsens, supplement treatment with:

- ☐ Good Cry
- ☐ Healing Touch
- ☐ Chill Pill
- ☐ Day Off
- ☐ Retail Therapy
- ☐ Field Trip

Doctor's Note

1. MEDIA MEDITATION
   - IMMERSION: SOAK IN MEDIA STREAM (DECADENT, DELIGHTFUL, AND FUN)
   - HOMEOPATHIC: CONSUME A SHORT FILM, POEM, OR PIN ON PINTEREST.
2. SOUND BATH
   - LISTEN TO MUSIC, MAKE MUSIC, OR ATTEND A SOUND BATH.
   - CREATE YOUR OWN "WALK-UP MUSIC." PLAY THE HYPE MUSIC BEFORE YOU WRITE.
3. TERRA THERAPY
   - SPEND TIME LOOKING AT CLOUDS, STAR GAZING, OR WATCH THE SUNSET.
   - TRY FOREST BATHING, HIKING, OR VISIT A BEACH, GARDEN, OR NATURE PRESERVE.
4. ART THERAPY
   - GOOF AROUND WITH A DIFFERENT ART MEDIUM: PAINTING, CRAFTING, CALLIGRAPHY.
   - GATHER A BANK OF IMAGES THAT INSPIRE AND COLLAGE.
5. LOTIONS AND POTIONS
   - INDULGE IN A BUBBLE BATH, FACE MASK, A MANI-PEDI, MASSAGE, OR HOT TUB SOAK.

Side effects may include: joy, serenity, inspiration, laughter, inner bliss, creative flow.

Uses: writer's block, premise envy, plot allergies, congestive art failure, creative constipation, story dysmorphia, protective author syndrome, character detachment disorder, general funk, malaise, art-thritis dialogue diarrhea, completion phobia, itchy cliché, bacterial backstory, cracked motive, superlative fever, analogy ulcers, chronic indecision, goal stones, obsessive confusion disorder, bloated scene, style decay, conflict sores, loss of senses, thematic anemia, inflammation of the inner Critic, mild-to-moderate procrastination, resolution aphasia, hematone, hypo-POV, bacterial mansplaining, gastro-trite-ice, doubt, chronic idea overwhelm, muse-on-pause.

If condition persists, seek a story professional.

Sascha Brown Rice
Signature

Let it Go

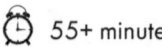 55+ minutes

It's hard to know when to hold on and when to let go. Do you need a break, or is it time to buckle down? Where should you put your attention? What can you let go of?

Step 1. Put your cards on the table. 15 minutes

Use list making to identify your options, obstacles, and opportunities.

- ☐ If you're trying to decide which project to prioritize, list the options.
  - List the various projects.
  - List the possible permutations and next steps.

- ☐ List the obstacles and opportunities.
  - What are your expectations?
  - What's tripping you up?
  - What are you afraid of?
  - What are you hoping for?
  - What does your critic have to say?

Tip: If the critic has a nagging question, just jot it down on your question list. This way, your critic will feel confident it won't be forgotten, and you can focus on the big picture.

Step 2. Wander and walk away. 24-72 hours

Calibrate with a dose of Story RX. The Collaborate Cycle is all about connection. Bask in the sunshine of love and leisure. Reset with connection.

- ☐ Walk away.
  Even if for one day, put the project to the side. If possible, take a few days off.

- ☐ Wander.
  - Take yourself on an artist date.
  - Spend time in nature and with friends.

Step 3. Review and reflect. 20 minutes

Revisit the cards on the table. Now that you've taken time to recharge, reconsider the options, opportunities, and obstacles.

- ☐ Ask, *What am I making it mean?*
  - Sometimes the issue isn't the issue.
  - Lean into the emotion and ask, What am I making it mean?

- ☐ Is the noise the critic's making even related to your project?
    - Is the material triggering an old trauma?
    - Look at the context. Is the critic responding to something in real life?
        Ask, Is something happening with my health, the weather, the world, or a family member?

- ☐ Ask, *Do I agree?*
    - Is that a valid concern? Is it something to consider later?
    - What if everything you're doing is fine?
        - What if your pace is perfect? What if you are exactly right on schedule? What if you aren't doing anything wrong? What if you aren't lacking? What if you have what you need?

Step 4. Discard.   10 minutes

- ☐ What can you let go of?
    Shed and release options, opportunities, or obstacles.
    - Let go of an idea.
    - Let go of the timeline.
    - Let go of the relationship.
    - Let go of the reward.
    - Let go of the feeling.
    - Let go of an outcome.

Step 5. Ask *how,* not *if . . .*   10 minutes

- ☐ Ask, *How can I resolve this?*
    If it's time to suit up, then don't get mad at the rain; grab some gear.
    - What do you need?
    - Do you need support? Call in a mentor or the muse.

- ☐ Assess your capacity.
    - Look at your calendar and see what's possible now.
    - How many hours per week can you dedicate to your writing practice?
    - Be conservative. It's better to under-promise and over-deliver.

- ☐ Look at the next two weeks and identify pockets of time.
- ☐ Add these writing sessions to your calendar.
    Even if you only plan to write for ten or fifteen minutes, make an appointment and add that to your schedule.
    * *Be realistic. Consider work, family, health, and recreation.*

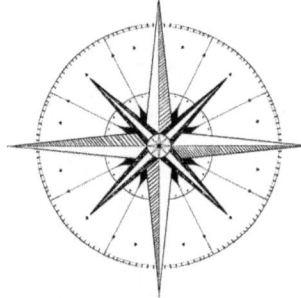

PART IV

Craft

THE FALL CYCLE

Chapter Thirteen: Revision
- ☐ Pick a Process
- ☐ The End
- ☐ Timeline

Chapter Fourteen: The Best Story Structure
- ☐ Your Cup of Tea
- ☐ Five Sequences

Chapter Fifteen: Point of View
- ☐ Story Sip
- ☐ Mini Masterclass
- ☐ POV Shake-Up

Chapter Sixteen: The Messy Middle
- ☐ Destination
- ☐ I'm Done!

Calibrate Your Compass

Tidy up: Declutter for ten minutes.
- ☐ Clear away debris, salvage scraps, and take inventory.
- ☐ One writer's trash is another writer's treasure. (Refer to the mosaic method.)

CHAPTER THIRTEEN

Revision

Fall: Before the rewards of the harvest, we review, revise, and refine.
The Craft Cycle is a time of turning and returning.

RECAP: Drafting

In this chapter, we focus on the editing process and the different types of revision. We also break down the two main approaches to drafting: plotting and pantsing. To liberate ourselves from the conventional constraints of outlining, we look at the spine of your story.

Tools and Techniques

- ◎ Pantsers and plotters
- ◎ The mosaic method
- ◎ Story spine

Chapter Thirteen Activities

Pick a process.

15 minutes

What's your natural tendency? Are you a pantser, a plotter, or something in between?

- ☐ Use freewriting to reflect on your process.
    - Do you need to see the plot before you begin, or do you prefer to write your way to clarity?
    - Do you like ideation or prefer getting down to brass tacks?
    - Do you delight in unexpected discoveries or avoid improvisation?
    - Do you prefer following a roadmap or wandering?

- ☐ Review and reflect.
    - Reread your writing. Are you a pantser or a plotter?
    - You don't have to fit in a box. Consider coming up with your own moniker.

_____

_____

_____

_____

_____

_____

_____

_____

The End

⏰ 20 minutes

Rather than thinking your way to an ending, try writing your way to it. Even if you have no idea how the piece will wrap up, give it a go. Make your best effort to bring the story to a close. Let go of pretty and simply try to resolve all the through lines. If you simply can't get words onto the page, try dictating an ending. Recording can free you up from getting it just right.

Step 1. Key into the emotional tone of the finale.   6 minutes

- ☐ Make a list of emotions that you'd like the audience/reader to feel.
  Consult emotion list from Chapter Five.

- ☐ Describe the tone of the ending.
  - Is it happy or sad?
  - Comedic or tragic?
  - Tidy or mysterious?

Step 2. Next, use list making or word clouds to brainstorm.   4 minutes

- ☐ Make a list of possible endings.
  - Challenge yourself to think of at least ten possible endings and be sure to have at least three really stupid ideas.
  - Consider what's lost, found, discovered, learned, revealed, destroyed . . .

Step 3. Pick an ending, set a timer, and give it a go.   5 minutes

- ☐ Sketch the ending. It can be a super messy brainstorm.

Step 4. Review and reflect.   5 minutes

- ☐ Read through what you've written and look for clues. Was there anything that felt close or important?

Repeat as necessary.

_____

_____

_____

_____

Timeline

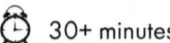 30+ minutes

Find your way to (or way back to) structure. Stories can span generations, or they can be contained to a single day. Before you sculpt the arc of your story, simply plot the key events. Then map out your story's events in chronological order.

☐ Use list making to brainstorm the events in your main character's journey and the key events in the story.

> For this exercise, include even events outside the timeline of the story like birth and death; milestones, like a graduation, a beginning or end of a romantic relationship, a marriage, a divorce, a new job, a move; hardships, like illness, injury, or loss; turning points, like a discovery, an epiphany, etc.

☐ After you've made the list, create a chronological timeline.

☐ Next, circle the section of the timeline covered in your story.

☐ Now look over the timeline and use freewriting to explore what you notice.

- Are there surprises?
- Is there a missing setup or payoff?
- Is there something implied that needs to be included in the story?
- Is there something in the story that could be implied instead?
- Look for the peaks and valleys. What are the high points and what are the low points?

Tip: Make the process tactile and take up space. Consider using sticky notes or index cards. Spread out on the floor or use a whiteboard. This makes it easy to play with sequences and takes away the pressure of putting events in the perfect spot.

_____

_____

_____

_____

_____

_____

Calibrate Your Compass

Go nuts: When the Craft Cycle make you crazy, let yourself go nuts.
☐ Move your body: Crank some music and take a ten-minute dance party break.

CHAPTER FOURTEEN

The Best Story Structure

Fall: Before the harvest, tend the garden. Weed and water.

RECAP: Beat By Beat

In this chapter, we began with a brief survey of popular narrative structures, then explored an intuitive approach to structure with the five sequences. Each sequence is anchored in a sensory beat. We build the story beat by beat. Find a structure that works for you.

Tools and Techniques

- ◎ The beating heart
- ◎ Story beats
- ◎ The five sequences

Chapter Fourteen Activities

Your Cup of Tea

🕐 20 minutes

What's your cup of tea? What type of stories do you prefer? Sip and study.

- ☐ Make yourself a cup of tea.
- ☐ Use list making to jot down some of your favorite books, movies, or series.
  - It doesn't need to be your ultimate top ten. Simply list ten stories that you love or wish you had written.
- ☐ Use freewriting to explore what these stories have in common.
- ☐ Read and reflect.
  - Is there a common theme, genre, character, or narrative style that appeals to you?

_____

_____

_____

_____

_____

_____

_____

_____

_____

_____

The Five Sequences

We build the story beat by beat:

1. OUCH!
2. OH NO!
3. POP!
4. UH OHHH!
5. AAAAH!

Download
Five Sequences Beat Sheet

Five Sequences

To discover the spine of your story, first find the five key sequences.

    1: OUCH!   Opening situation and catalyst

    2: OH NO!   Hero faces life-changing obstacle

    3: POP!   Challenges build to a climax

    4: UH OHHH!   Challenges get worse, but protagonist continues to pursue the goal

    5: AAAAH!   Success or defeat

Step 1: Where does the main character begin?

Use freewriting to explore where your character begins and what they want. What would your character's ordinary world look and feel like?

Tip: Identify the root action at the heart of their goal. Michael Hauge breaks all goals into one of these four categories: to win, to stop, to escape, to retrieve.

Step 2: What stands in their way?

Use list making or word clouds to brainstorm possible obstacles the character might face.

Step 3: What is at stake?

Use freewriting to explore these questions:

- What is at stake?
- What does the character fear losing?
- What will she gain or lose?
- What would amp up the tension?
- What might lock the main character in the predicament?

Step 4: Where does your character end?

Use freewriting, word clouds, or list making to explore where your character ends.

Consider these questions:

- How does the story end? Victory or defeat?
- What do they win or lose?
- What have they learned? What have they gained?
- How have they changed?

Step 5: Synthesize.

After exploring the four guiding questions, review your writing and do your best to sketch five key beats.

- You may not have unearthed the exact structure. Even so, take your best guess at identifying five starter beats.
- Bridge: What questions feel unanswered?
- Record insights about your process and any new takeaways about story structure in your Field Notes Writing Tracker.

 Download
The Five Sequence Template

⊘ Calibrate Your Compass

Back to school: Take a trip to the library and check out some books.
☐ Read around your story. Pick books related to the setting or your character's hobbies or emotional problems. Find stories covering the same time period or that are told in a similar way. Visit the young adult nonfiction section. How do authors explain your topic to kids?

Point of View

Fall: The Craft Cycle heralds the harvest.
Give thanks and honor those who have gone before.

RECAP: Your Voice

Each writer has a unique voice. In this chapter, we review how point of view can shape the reader's experience. A story can be told from a variety of perspectives, and each angle triggers different emotions for the reader. The author decides whose eyes we see the world through. We look at examples because rereading our favorites illuminates how it's done.

Tools and Techniques

- Voice
- Point of view
- Breaking the fourth wall

Chapter Fifteen Activities

Story sip.

🕐 15 minutes

You don't need to reread a whole book or chew through an entire season's worth of scripts. Take sips. Study and savor.

Step 1. Pick a text.

☐ Pick a text that's interesting to you or pick one of the examples excerpted in this chapter.

Step 2. Focus your attention.

☐ Focus your attention on a specific aspect of the craft and analyze it.

- You may examine how the author builds worlds, crafts character descriptions, makes transitions, uses dialogue, or shifts between perspectives.

Step 3. Review and reflect.

☐ Write about what you notice in your journal.

_____

_____

_____

_____

_____

_____

_____

_____

_____

Mini Masterclass

 45 minutes

You don't need to reread a whole book or chew through an entire season's worth of scripts. Take sips. Study and savor.

Step 1. Pick a text.
- ☐ Pick a text that is relevant to what you're writing (e.g., short story, essay, poem).
  - Select a text that's interesting to you. If you're writing an essay, read essays. If you're penning a memoir, get your hands on memoirs. If you're writing a script, round up screenplays.

Step 2. Focus your attention.
- ☐ Focus your attention on a specific aspect of the craft and analyze it.
  - You may examine how the author builds worlds, crafts character descriptions, makes transitions, uses dialogue, or shifts between perspectives.

  Tip: Make it easy and use the text examples in this chapter.

Step 3. Review and reflect.
In your journal, write about what you notice.
- ☐ How does it make you feel? What do you experience?

Tension	Intrigue	Romantic
Intimacy	Immediacy	Immersive
Empathy	Comedy	Fear

- ☐ Here are other questions to consider:
  - If you look at voice, ask:
    - Is it first person or third person?
    - Objective or subjective?
    - Is the narrator reliable?
    - Why do you think the author chose this point of view?
    - What if the author chose to use first instead of third person? Third instead of second? And so on.
    - How does the voice connect to the themes of the story?
  - If you focus on the dialogue, ask:
    - Is this dialogue moving us forward? What would happen if the author had taken out this line of dialogue? How would this affect the rest of the narrative?
    - When and why does the author use dialogue?

_____

_____

_____

_____

_____

_____

_____

_____

_____

_____

_____

_____

_____

_____

Ready to go further?

☐ Study one specific element and compare authors.
  • Study the first paragraph of different books and see how the author approaches beginnings.
  • Read the last few pages of a book to see how the author wraps the narrative.

POV Shake-Up

 15 minutes

A great way to find drama is to shift the point of view. Drop your character into an unexpected situation, explore what-ifs, or send them into a bizarre situation. Spend some quality time with your character.

Step 1: Warm-up   3 minutes
Freewrite from a different point of view. Goof around.
Select an animal or object. Write from that perspective.
- ☐ What do you want, fear, love, crave? Who are your friends? Enemies?
- ☐ Examples: a ring, a piece of trash, a streetlamp, a watch, a piano, a sock, an iPhone, a key, a dog, a bird, a pet, a bomb, a cake, a lake, a step, a closet, a ball, a superhero, a magical creature, etc.

Step 2: Pick a new POV.   1 minute
- ☐ Examples: a teenager, a detective, a criminal, your mother, a dad, a baby, a grandmother, a character from a movie

Step 3: Now describe a familiar event from this new POV.   4 minutes
- ☐ Examples: eating breakfast, driving to work, cooking, kissing, going to the gym

Step 4: Repeat step three, using your main character.   7 minutes
- ☐ Consider the following questions:
  - How does the world look from the new POV?
  - What does your character want?
  - Is there something they love that you hate (or vice versa)?
  - Is there something they fear that's ordinary to you?
  - How does the world look, smell, taste, feel, sound . . . ?
  - Who are the character's friends? Enemies?
- ☐ Bridge: Jot down takeaways from the writing session.
  - What did you learn about your character?
  - Did you discover a new secret or fear?
  - What surprised you?
  - Did you knock up against a new question?
- ☐ Field Notes
  - Did you learn anything about your process? What came up?

Note: The objective of this exercise might feel unclear. That's okay! If you feel disoriented, good! The point is to shake up your thinking so you can access the subconscious. Trust you will find insights into what the character is thinking and feeling.

For example, one student was struggling with a character that was silent and stoic. The momentum of the story was dragging. I suggested she force her characters to deal with an overflowing plumbing problem. This got the quiet character talking. Finally, the writer understood what was going on with him and how to move the story forward. This exercise revealed a betrayal he'd been hiding, and the drama took off. She even decided to keep the scene.

_____

_____

_____

_____

_____

_____

_____

_____

_____

_____

_____

_____

Calibrate Your Compass

Turn over a new leaf: Just because you haven't finished yet doesn't mean you can't finish. It may be time for a change. Calibrate with a pause.

☐ Reconsider your priority. What's the next best step?

The Messy Middle

Fall: When the Craft Cycle arrives, it's time to dump the excess.
To complete, we must also let go.

RECAP: Word by Word

One of the most difficult tasks for writers is completing a project. Finding the right way to wrap up a story can be genuinely baffling, but if you find yourself toggling between possibilities and stuck in a loop of endless pondering, the critic might be running the show. To make it to the finish line, the writer must be willing to change.

Tools and Techniques

- ◎ The messy middle
- ◎ The mists of maybe
- ◎ Transformation
- ◎ Land the plane

Chapter Sixteen Activities

Destination

⏰ 15 minutes

Declutter your mind and reevaluate the goal.
- ☐ Use freewriting and list making to capture what's floating around in your head.
  - – Write down the questions, worries, and possibilities.
  - – Include specific story questions, process issues, and outcome concerns.

- ☐ Make a question list.
  - – Review what you wrote and identify the burning issues. Add questions and decisions to your question list.

- ☐ Read and reflect.
  - – Did you change your goal without knowing it? And, if so, does that work?
  - – Is it time to revise the goal? Do you need more time, or are you changing direction?
  - – Does your goal still match your why?

_____

_____

_____

_____

_____

_____

_____

_____

_____

I'm done!

Visualize what "done" looks like.

Step 1: Use freewriting to explore. Consider these guiding questions:

☐ What does completion look like?

- *What does "finishing" look like for me?*

- *How do I want to feel about it?*

- *What is enough?*

- *How will finishing change my life externally?*

- *How do I hope I will change internally?*

☐ Are there changes you fear or hope for?

- *What might I gain?*

- *What am I ready to let go of?*

- *How will this impact my relationships?*

- *Is there a transformation I'm seeking?*

- *Is there an experience I fear?*

Step 2: I am done!

☐ Congratulations! You did it!

- Even if you're not really done, let's pretend for an hour.

- Even if you haven't hit your original goal, it's important to acknowledge the work you have done, so let's practice.

- Even for just the next hour, decide it is time for you to walk away. Identify a marker or milestone and acknowledge your efforts.

Step 3: I have done enough.

Sometimes speaking can free up creativity.

☐ Say it out loud and see how it feels: I have done enough.

☐ Now write it in your journal: I have done enough.

☐ Use freewriting to explore the feelings that come up.

Step 4: Review and reflect.

☐ Read over your writing and record key observations in your journal or Field Notes Writing Tracker.

Step 5: Do something nice for yourself.

☐ How can you celebrate this milestone?

- Leave something wonderful for yourself to come back to in your notebook. Write yourself an encouraging note, transcribe an inspiring quote in your Field Notes Writing Tracker, add stickers to celebrate progress, or place a flower on your writing desk. Schedule an artist date.

- Give a gift to your future self. Challenge yourself to try a variety of rewards.

☐ Extra Credit: Give yourself permission to shine!

- Brag to a friend and observe how it feels.

  - Enlist a trusted friend and ask them if they wouldn't mind listening to you talk about your writing process.

  - Talk about what's going well with your process. Celebrate that you've found tools and techniques that work for you. Claim your victories.

- Use freewriting to explore the experience.

_____

_____

_____

_____

_____

_____

_____

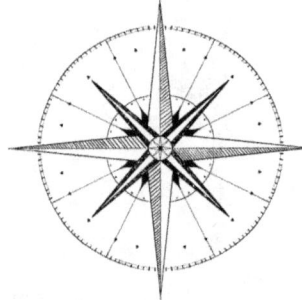

PART V

Dream to Draft

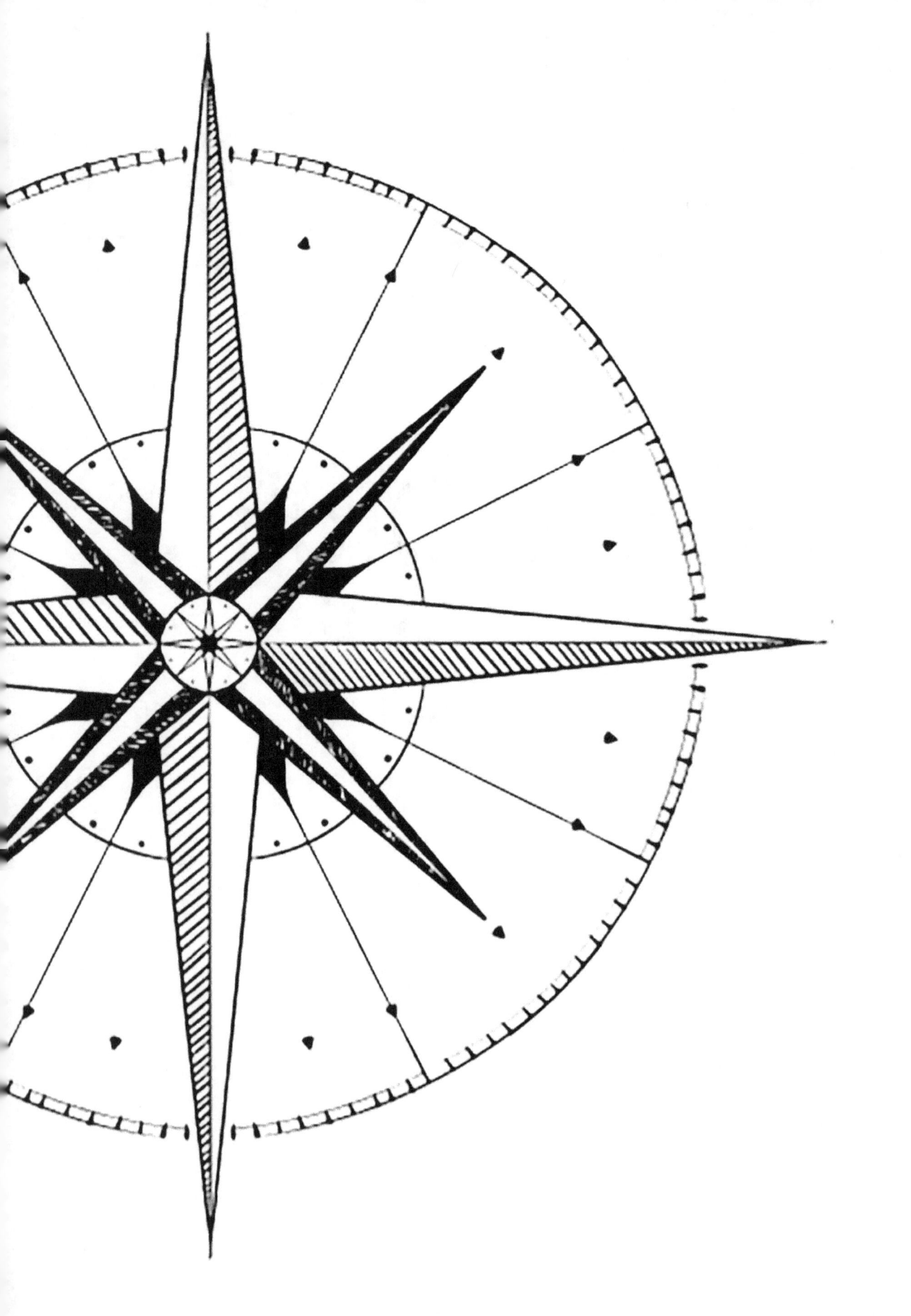

 Calibrate Your Compass

Consult your creative compass.
  ☐ You decide how to calibrate.

CHAPTER SEVENTEEN

Story Spirals

Dream, dare, and draft. Calibrate and begin again.

RECAP: Dare to Draft

To spiral through all the Story Cycles, remember to deploy the playful techniques of the Collaborate Cycle and the invigorating energy of the Cultivate Cycle. Employ letter writing to experience the world of the story from a fresh POV. A new vantage point helps you pull the work out your head and into the world. Letter writing can also help you connect to the character's inner world and your own psyche. By daring to dive into the river of emotions, you will be able to move from dream to draft.

Tools and Techniques

- ◎ Story spirals
- ◎ Connect with the audience
- ◎ Letter writing

 Download
All-Weather Playbook

Call in the Season

Story Cycles move in spirals. Circle back to the season whose energy you need.

- ◎ Calibrate with a wintry pause.
  - Include the bridge practice into your writing routine.
  - Invoke the Calibrate Cycle and reconnect with your *why*.

- ✿ Wake up by dipping into spring's well of mystery.
  - Plotting and planting take time, so move through the Cultivate Cycle by returning to the senses and emotions.
  - Calibrate with the question list and discovery writing.

- ☀ Restart by stoking your creative fire with collaboration.
  - Cozy up to your critic, call in your muse, and connect with your reader.
  - Spark the summer cycle with whimsy and play.

- ▲ Renew with radical self-care when the Craft Cycle tires you out.
  - The fall cycle offers a treasure trove of tools, but the harvest heralds transformation. To finally finish, you must be willing to let go.
  - Scaffold the process with radical self-care and enlist the kind critic.

_____

_____

_____

_____

_____

_____

_____

_____

STORY CYCLES: THE BREAKDOWN

CALIBRATE
QUIET, REST

Reconnect to Your Why

Bridge

Pause

CULTIVATE
PLAN, PLOT

Emotions and Senses

Discovery Writing

Question List

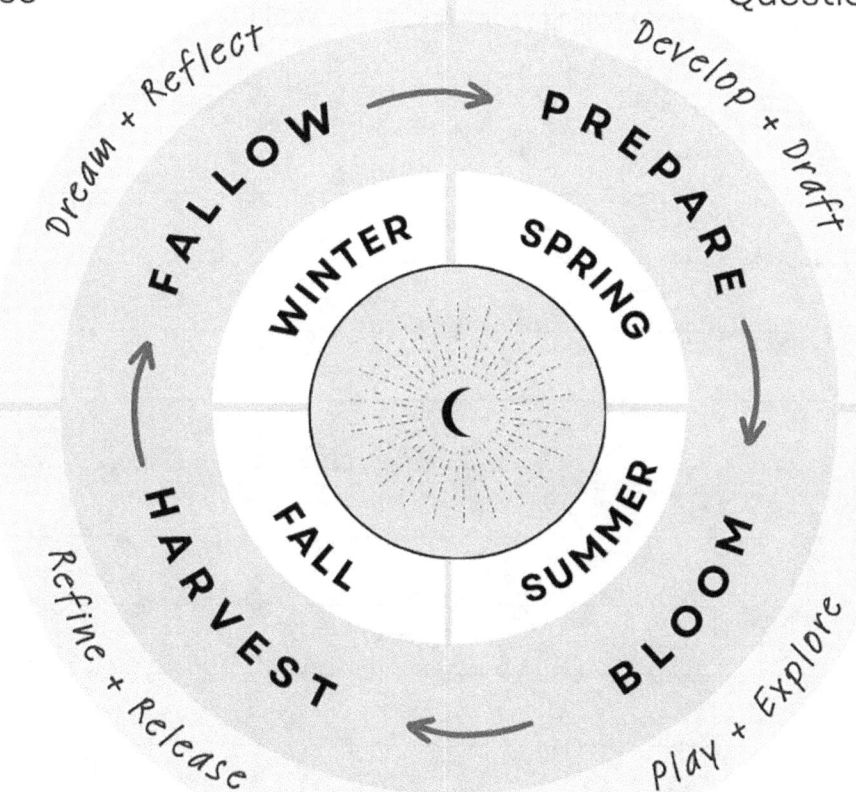

Dream + Reflect

Develop + Draft

FALLOW

PREPARE

WINTER

SPRING

FALL

SUMMER

HARVEST

BLOOM

Refine + Release

Play + Explore

Kind Critic

Love List

Feedback

REVISE, LET GO
CRAFT

Be Visible

Celebrate

Warm-Up

CONNECT, SHINE
COLLABORATE

Chapter Seventeen Activities

Thank You Note

🕐 30 minutes

Set aside time to write a thank you note to your muse. Sometimes it's hard to give ourselves credit for what we've done, so try looking at your writing from the point of view of your muse.

☐ In the letter, acknowledge what you've done and thank your muse for the inspiration and strength they provided to get you to this point.

☐ You can also ask for help putting your work into the world.

_____

_____

_____

_____

_____

_____

_____

_____

_____

_____

_____

Dear Me

Write a letter to your future self and tuck it away. Reconnect to curiosity, reset to a posture of play, and recapture a sense of wonder. Write a letter to yourself in your Field Notes Writing Tracker.

Consider these questions:

☐ What do you love about yourself that you always want to remember?

☐ When times are tough, whom can you reach out to?

☐ When times are great, whom can you celebrate with?

☐ What are telltale signs that the critic has shown up?

☐ If you had a secret message to yourself, what would it be?

☐ Clarify your why.

– Why do you want to tackle this story?

– Why you?

– Why now?

Add practical suggestions:

☐ Note three good places to write.

☐ Note the time of day that is most productive.

☐ Prescribe self-care, medicinal reading, or treats.

☐ Share inspiration: a favorite tip, mantra, quote, or insight.

Have fun with it. Try one of these suggested approaches:

• Make a request.

• Express appreciation.

• Reflect on your experience.

• Send an SOS to your muse.

• Write a love letter to yourself.

• Serve the critic a restraining order.

Shortcut: If you don't want to pen a long letter, make it easy.

☐ Jot down a few words in your Field Notes Writing Tracker.

☐ One word on a sticky note can be a bridge back to creativity.

☐ Dash off a postcard and pop it in the mail.

☐ Slip a sweet valentine into your journal.

Dear Reader . . .

 20 minutes

Imagine they just finished watching or reading your story. Consider their experience and what you want them to take away from your story. You might tell the reader why you decided to write the story, why it's important to you, and what you hope the reader will connect to. You don't actually send the letter to a reader but rather use the activity to reactivate your why and reconnect to the value in your work.

Tip: This is not a disclaimer; instead, this is a way to remember why you care.

Step 1. Imagine your reader.

☐ Use list making to describe your imagined reader.

- Before writing take a moment to envision a specific reader.
- Consider these attributes:
    - Age, gender, location, hobbies, dreams, challenges, secrets; what do they want, need, fear?

Step 2. Write the letter.

☐ As you write the letter, consider these questions:

- Why are you writing this story?
- Why do you care about these characters?
- What do you love about the world?
- What do you hope your reader learns from your story?
- What do you hope their key takeaways will be?
- What do you hope readers connect with and relate to?
- How do you hope your story will help the reader?
- Heal . . . move away from pain?
- Relief . . . move toward pleasure?

☐ Consider your approach:

- Share your enthusiasm.
- Make a request.
- Express appreciation.
- Send an invitation.

Step 3. Seal and reveal.

- ☐ Put the letter in an envelope, seal it, and tuck it away.
- ☐ Wait a few days.
- ☐ Make yourself a cup of tea and read it.
- ☐ Write about your observations. What did the activity reveal?
  - Insights about your why?
  - Revelations about blocks?
  - Practical ways to navigate the next steps?

_____

_____

_____

_____

_____

_____

_____

_____

_____

_____

_____

_____

THE ELEMENTS: A GUIDE

Harness the elemental forces. This quick guide highlights when and why to employ each cycle's corresponding element.

 Calibrate: Activate the element of air: clarity.

   LACK: Lack of air can lead to feeling stuck.

   EXCESS: An excess of air can lead to overthinking, indecision, and disorientation.

 Cultivate: Activate the element of water: emotion.

   LACK: A lack of water makes the story, process, or mindset feel brittle.

   EXCESS: An excess of water can result in a feeling of overwhelm or drowning.

 Collaborate: Activate the element of fire: connection.

   LACK: A lack of fire leads to a cold, lifeless, or flat story.

   EXCESS: An excess of fire can lead to burnout or a dominance of anger and hate.

 Craft: Activate the element of earth: grounding.

   LACK: A lack of earth leaves a story without substance, meaning, or tangibility.

   EXCESS: An excess of earth can manifest as perfectionism, fear of being visible, or an inability to take risks.

CHAPTER EIGHTEEN

It's Elemental

*Tune In: Drop into the now. Take a breath. Activate a wintry pause.
Plunge into the potent waters of the spring cycle. Fire up inspiration
with the summer season. Get grounded with fall's earth energy.*

RECAP: Brave the Elements

In this chapter, we use the elemental properties of each Story Cycle to infuse the writing process with new life. We invoke the elements to rekindle a connection to our story and to penetrate one of craft's more nuanced fundamentals: theme. When a writer is unable to find solutions, it is time to call upon the elemental forces.

Tools and Techniques

- ◎ The elemental forces
- ◎ Calibrate: air
- ◎ Cultivate: water
- ◎ Collaborate: fire
- ◎ Craft: earth

ELEMENTAL

Let's break down each element's basic characteristics and show how the elements correspond to Story Cycles and seasons.

◎ **AIR:** This element corresponds to the power of the mind.
- Air corresponds to winter and the techniques of the Calibrate Cycle.
- When a writer feels stuck, the airy act of calibration can lighten and open possibilities.
- Air wakes up clarity, communication, and expression.

❀ **WATER:** This element is about emotion.
- Water energy is the hallmark of spring and the lifeblood of the Cultivate Cycle.
- When a writer feels disconnected, the watery nature of cultivating can activate emotion, intuition, and healing.
- Water brings the writer flow and adaptability.

☼ **FIRE:** This element represents passion and creativity.
- Summer pulses with fiery energy, fueling the Collaborate Cycle.
- When a writer is unable to make progress, it's time to ignite creativity by unleashing fiery tactics.
- Fire acts as a cleanser to burn up negative thoughts, and the heat can rekindle connection.

▲▲ **EARTH:** This element corresponds to practical and physical features.
- This grounding force is rooted in the Craft Cycle and heralds fall's harvest.
- The treasure trove of earthy tools gives both the writer and the project structure.
- Earth acts as a calming and grounding force.

Download
The Elements: A Complete Guide

Chapter Eighteen Activities

In Your Element

🕐 25 minutes

Shift the energy. Use the elements to activate the power of Story Cycles. Follow your intuition.

Step. 1. Diagnose the condition that ails your story.   3 minutes

- ☐ Identify which area or aspect of the process you'd like to focus on.

- ☐ Use list making to brainstorm key characters, key moments, and/or important sequences. (List at least five but no more than fifteen.)

Step 2: Pick one area and explore with freewriting.   5 minutes

- ☐ What emotions does this facet of the story elicit?

- ☐ What emotions are you trying to invoke in the story and in the reader?

- ☐ How would you describe the tone and mood surrounding these details?

- ☐ Consider the senses:
  - Is it sweet, slow, loud, soft, fast, funky, ethereal, or grand?
  - Is it light, dark, silly, sad, patriotic, or mysterious?

Step 3. Describe what ails you and/or your story.   5 minutes

- ☐ Use freewriting to clarify the issue.
  - How would you describe the problem?
  - Use the senses to characterize the issue.
  - Is there an excess or a lack?

Step 4: Pick which element can help energize your process.   4 minutes

Step 5: Pick the Story Cycle that's right for you.   8 minutes

Option A: Calibrate—Clear the Air
Take a field trip to the bookstore or do some armchair investigation.

Option B: Cultivate—That's My Theme Song
Use music to create a temporary score for your story.

Option C: Collaborate—Get Fired Up
Use freewriting to explore desire. Turn the heat up and give the desire a sinful spin.

Option D: Craft—Down to Earth
Come down to earth with a small act of self-care.

Option A: Calibrate—Clear the Air

Take a field trip to the bookstore or do some armchair investigation. The way other projects are marketed can help you clear the air. Go to the bookstore and see where books are shelved. Alternatively, look at a streaming service like Netflix and note how they describe shows.

Step 1: Find five books or shows that are in some way comparable to your story.

Step 2: Use list making to record your discoveries.
- What categories are you drawn to?
- Which sections might be where your book is shelved?
- Which area can you imagine your project fitting into?

You can look at online booksellers to see how they categorize books. For example, in the category of memoir and biography, one online seller lists these subcategories:

- Adventure
- Explorers & Survival
- Art & Literature
- Cultural & Regional
- Diaries & Memoirs
- Historical
- LGBTQ+
- Politics & Activism
- Professional
- Academic
- Religious
- Sports
- True Crime
- Women

On streaming services, notice how the mood is distilled into two or three words, like these examples:
- soapy, slow burn
- Surreal thriller, cozy mystery
- intimate, quirky
- cerebral, drama

Step 3: Use freewriting to clear the air.
- ☐ How would you categorize your project?
- ☐ What are three words you would use to describe your show or book?

Note: It's okay if there are multiple moods or categories. We're seeing more hybrid genres like horror-comedy, mystery-romance, or detective sci-fi.

Ready to go further?

Listen to the score of the television shows or movies you picked. Borrow their theme song!

Option B: Cultivate—That's My Theme Song

Just as filmmakers use music to cue the audience, we can use music to shift or heighten our emotional landscape. Tap into the vast body of music available and borrow a "theme song" or create a temporary score for your story. What if you had theme music for your story? Would it be light, dark, silly, sad, or mysterious?

> Step 1: Pick comps.
> Write down five comparable projects. Most importantly, think of comps that have a similar mood or tone. These can include a movie, a series, an opera, or even a video game.

> Step 2: Research and pull selects.
> Now scour the web for soundtracks and the musical scores of the titles you have identified. Pull large selections of possible tracks. Gather a grab bag of possibilities: consider your characters, specific scenes, or key sequences.

> Step 3: Pick a theme song or soundtrack.
> Pick a theme song or string together five or more tracks to create a temporary score for your story.

Option C: Collaborate—Fired Up

Use freewriting to explore desire. Turn the heat up and give the desire a sinful spin.

> Step 1. Pick an emotion that drives your character's desire.
> Consult the feelings list in Chapter Five to identify a core emotion at play.

> Step 2. Explore the sinful side of their desire and write from the POV of your main character.
> Prompt: *I want . . .*

> Tip: Consider the Seven Deadly Sins for inspiration:
> GREED: Characters want more.
> LUST: Characters want sex.
> ENVY: Characters want what other people have.
> PRIDE: Characters value themselves and want to feel as if they're worth something.
> SLOTH: Characters just want to do nothing.
> WRATH: Characters want to cause suffering.
> GLUTTONY: Characters just want to consume.

> Step 3. Use freewriting to explore how this desire shows up in your story.
> Prompt: *This story is really about . . .*

Option D: Craft—Down to Earth

Come down to earth with a small act of self-care.

Step 1. Consult your self-care cheat sheet from Chapter Two.
- Consider the eight realms.

Step 2. Pick a tiny, easy, free action.
- Stop and smell the flowers.
- Look at the moon, watch the clouds go by, or close your eyes and listen.
- Feel your feet on the earth; let the sun kiss your skin.
- Take a walk in the woods or sit in the shade of a tree.
- Get outside. Experience the elements!

Step 3: Now get outdoors and connect with Mother Nature!

Note: No need to drop money on a spa day. Steer clear of fancy and go for free.

_____

_____

_____

_____

_____

_____

_____

_____

_____

_____

Story Cycle Writing Playlist

Desert Soundscape	Desert wind and critters
Search, Fight, Win	Driving, battle, triumph, grand, intense
Swoon Romantic	Hopeful, longing, romantic, heart strings
Dark and Stormy	Dark, intense, foreboding, looming
Moody Mood Music	Ethereal, moody, hopeful, possibility, mystery

Download
Story Cycle Playlists

Ready to go further?

Create a mixtape for your character.

- What songs would be on their mixtape?
  - For example, for a project set in the '90s, I created a playlist of pop songs my character would find on the radio during that period. Even if she didn't like the song, it provoked a reaction and revealed more of her personality.
- Is your story set in a specific period?
  - Find pop hits that transport you to the show's era.
- Is your story set in nature?
  - Ocean waves, desert wind, jungle rain . . . Cue up a soundscape!
- Need inspiration? Try a Story Cycle Playlist.

 Calibrate Your Compass

Consult your creative compass.

☐ You decide how to calibrate.

Collaborate with the Critic

*Craft: During the hard work of the harvest, the critic likes
to turn up the heat. When the critic stirs up fear and doubt,
cycle back to summer and collaborate with the critic.*

RECAP: Moving Forward

In this chapter, we expose the critic's greatest hits and provide ways to reframe their complaints. Rather than hiding from the critic, we consider their point of view and focus on building a relationship with them. To keep moving forward on the writing journey, we reassess expectations, learn how to agree to disagree, and when to stage an intervention.

Tools and Techniques

- ◎ Reframe
- ◎ Agree to disagree
- ◎ Critic's tricks and greatest hits
- ◎ Impact statement

Chapter Nineteen Activities

Suggestion Box

🕐 30 minutes

Let the critic know you're taking their concerns under consideration.

- ☐ Explore with freewriting.
  - Find out what's worrying them.
- ☐ Read and review.
  - What does the critic need?
- ☐ Make an adjustment.
  - Give them a treat, make an artist date, or assign them a job.
- ☐ Set up a "suggestion box."
  - Designate a spot in your Field Notes Writing Tracker for the critic to make suggestions.

_____

_____

_____

_____

_____

_____

_____

_____

_____

_____

FLIP THE SCRIPT: Five Reframes to Quiet the Critic

Turn the critic's complaints around.

1. Consider the possibility that you are exactly where you need to be.
   - What if the real problem is the critic's bad attitude?

     Reframe:

     > What if I am on the right path?
     > What if I'm not doing anything wrong?
     > What if my pace is perfect?

2. Challenge the veracity of the critic's complaints.
   - Is the content of the complaint the real issue?

     Reframe:

     > Why is this an issue?
     > Why is it a problem?

3. Look at what's driving the critic's panic.
   - What are they afraid might happen?

     Reframe:
   - Maybe the critic is worried you'll publish the messy first draft.
     - Promise you won't send out the work until you've brought them back for the revision process.
   - Maybe the critic feels unappreciated?
     - Give the critic a treat, make an artist date, or assign them a job!

4. Examine what you are making the critic's complaint mean.
   - What if the scary feelings you're having are actually good?

     Reframe:

     > What if I feel fear because I am sensitive and thoughtful?
     > What if I doubt the idea because I'm tired from working hard?
     > What if I feel worried because this matters to me?
     > What if I focus on faults because I care about the impact of my writing?

5. Get to know the critic's greatest hits.
   - Have you heard this story before?

     Reframe:

     > What if this is an old, toxic narrative?

Impact Statement

 60 minutes

Before you can really cozy up to the critic, take time to acknowledge how they've affected you. Write a letter to the critic that details how their attitude and behavior have impacted you.

WARNING: If you don't feel like you know the critic, go back to "Capture the Critic" (in Chapter Eight). Naming the critic is a pre-requisite for this exercise. Especially if your critic is based on some-body you know, be sure you've separated them from the real person.

Step 1: Before writing your impact statement, use freewriting to get your feelings out.
   Tip: This first draft is an uncensored rant that you don't "send."
   ☐ Detail how the critic's attitude has impacted you.
   ☐ Cite how the critic's messages have affected your mental and emotional health.
   - Be honest but remember that the critic is not on trial.
   - Remember, this is not about collecting evidence to prove your point.
   - You are building a relationship.
   ☐ Focus on a few meaningful examples.
   - If you find yourself condemning the critic or falling into self-pity, bring it back to specific messages from the critic.
   - Don't get stuck in the past.
   - Resist the urge to make an exhaustive list of every grievance through the ages. While you may have lots of examples, rehashing the past undermines your objective.

Step 2: Now cherry-pick the material for the impact statement.
   ☐ Let the critic know you understand that this is their job.
   ☐ Thank them for their care and concern.
   - Show love, respect, and gratitude.
   - Tell them you appreciate their interest in your writing.
   - If you have a tumultuous relationship, try to think back to a happier time when fear wasn't running the critic.
   ☐ List two or three specific traits or moments that exemplify their positive side. *(Don't be overly flattering or insincere; lack of sincerity will derail the intervention. The critic usually has a highly effective BS detector.)*
   - To encourage the critic to be more respectful, you need to demonstrate kindness and respect and be willing to hear out the critic.

Step 3: Make a request.
- ☐ Give them a job.
  - What's your critic's superpower? Is it research, proofreading, revision, analyzing, watching, or reading?
  - My critic loves tracking and ticking off items on a to-do list. I oblige but also make it fun for me with stickers and colored pens.

Step 4: Set the ground rules and clarify expectations.
- ☐ Offer the critic time and space to air their concerns. (Schedule it.)
- ☐ Define their area, (when, how, where, and what is fair game).
- ☐ Give the critic some love, like a treat, or schedule an artist date.

Step 5. End on a kind note.
- ☐ Reaffirm your love.
- ☐ Thank them for looking out for you.

Reminder: It's the critic's job to protect you, so you can set parameters, but you cannot—nor is it advisable to—eliminate all fear.

_____

_____

_____

_____

_____

_____

_____

_____

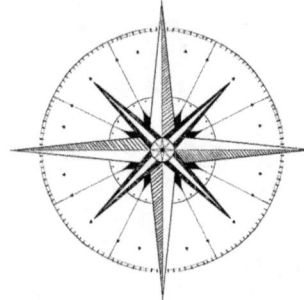

PART VI

That's a Wrap

 Calibrate Your Compass

Consult your creative compass.
- ☐ You decide how to calibrate.

Mulch More

Every Story Has A Season: Welcome the in-between time.
Progress, not perfection.

RECAP: Track the Process

A writer might be accustomed to tracking progress, but the Story Cycle Method illuminates the power of tracking the process and celebrating with treats. This chapter reveals the importance of feeding the muse and reiterates the importance of planning rest stops and scenic views.

Tools and Techniques

- Match your markers and milestones
- Rest stops and scenic views
- Progress, not perfection
- Feed the muse

Chapter Twenty Activities

Make an Offering

🕐 30+ minutes

While all exercises are optional, learning to acknowledge even little successes is essential.

- ☐ Honor your muse with a gift.

  - You might place a flower on your desk, go on an artist date, or break out that fancy journal you've been saving.

Note: For some, celebrating may feel highly uncomfortable, and for others, celebrating comes a little too naturally! It's worth taking time to observe your tendency.

Story Cycle Markers

When you map your journey, be prepared to spiral through the Story Cycles multiple times. Tune into the seasonal demands and include activities that celebrate the work of all cycles. Plot your course with markers that honor all of the seasons of creativity.

- ◎ Build in radical self-care, rest, and reflection. Calibrate with a pause.
  - Markers may include tasking yourself with freewrites that connect to your *why* and journaling to reflect on the process.
- ❀ Embrace the Cultivate Cycle's mindset of discovery. Track tasks centered on plotting and planning, like sowing seeds in the springtime.
  - Markers might include drafting an outline, reading a book on story structure, or doing research.
- ☀ Nourish your work with the spirit of play. The Collaborate Cycle reminds us to celebrate and connect to joy.
  - Schedule time for an artist date, connect with your muse, have tea with your critic, and celebrate a milestone.
- ▲ Go word by word, scene by scene. During the Craft Cycle, we revise and refine.
  - Count words and pages or liberate yourself from oppressive demands and simply track time spent. Focus on one element at a time: a scene, a character, structure, dialogue, etc.

_____

_____

_____

_____

_____

_____

_____

Match Your Markers and Milestones

🕐 1 hour +

Match your markers and milestones to the Story Cycle. Then, once you identify the next step on your writing journey, track the process, and then celebrate.

Step 1: Identify the major milestones and markers.

- ☐ Use freewriting to identify milestones. Explore these questions:
  - Consider your ideal vision. Where would you be with your writing in five years?
  - In light of your vision, what should you focus on first?
  - What's the most important goal for the next twelve months?
- ☐ Consider which Story Cycle you are moving through. Include actions that reflect all Story Cycles and set milestones appropriate to where you are in the process.
- ☐ Identify five mini milestones on the way to that bigger goal.
  - What are the concrete action steps to reach that goal?
- ☐ Identify the measurable markers to reach those milestones.

Reminder: When setting milestones, be sure they are something you can control. Milestones should match actionable outcomes. For example, perhaps you dream of being a best-selling author, selling a script, or winning an award. These goals are mostly out of your hands. It's okay to dream but set milestones that don't rely on outside recognition or gatekeepers. Instead, chart your course with milestones you can execute. For example, consider concrete accomplishments: complete a first draft, give a draft to beta reader for notes, send a script to an agent, or submit an essay to a contest.

Step 2: Write and track.

Now that you've identified markers and milestones, it's time to get to work.

- ☐ Write!
- ☐ Take time to regularly calibrate.
  - I like to use a writing tracker to chart the markers on the way to each milestone. The Field Notes Writing Tracker is also a good place to write down reflections, insights, and questions.

Step 3: Celebrate milestones.

Make time to acknowledge process.

Calibrate, then return to Step 1.

STORY CYCLE MARKERS

FALLOW, QUIET, REST

Reconnect to Your Why

Bridge

Pause

PLAN, PLOT, PREPARE

Emotions and Senses

Discovery Writing

Question List

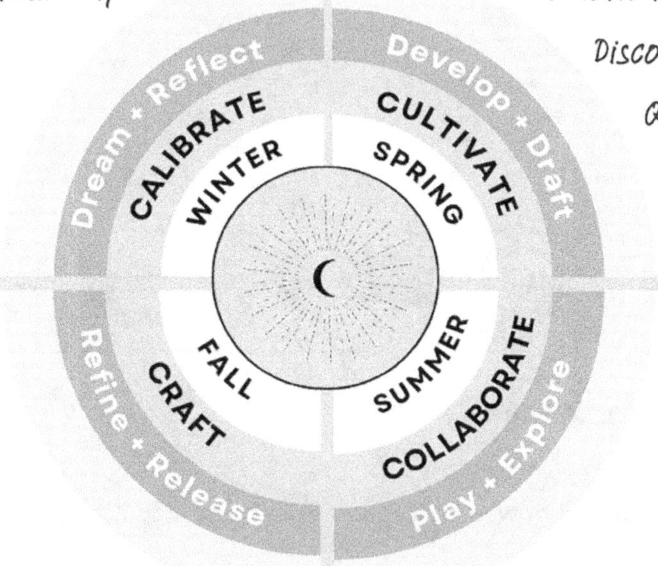
Dream + Reflect
CALIBRATE
WINTER
Develop + Draft
CULTIVATE
SPRING
Play + Explore
COLLABORATE
SUMMER
Refine + Release
CRAFT
FALL

Kind Critic

Love List

Feedback

REVISE, HARVEST LET GO

Be Visible

Celebrate

Warm-Up

BLOOM, SHINE CONNECT

Download
Story Cycle Markers

 Calibrate Your Compass

Consult your creative compass.
☐ You decide how to calibrate.

Take Away

In Season: Trust the process. You're right where you need to be.

- ◎ The airy stillness of winter's Calibrate Cycle requires patience.
- ❦ The watery, fertile Cultivate Cycle calls for faith.
- ☀ The fiery Collaborate Cycle calls for spontaneity and surrendering to the unknown.
- ▲ Fall's earthy Craft Cycle demands dedication and decisive action.

RECAP: The Long View

Remember, the closer we get to the finish line, the louder the critic might become. Writing can create powerful emotions for both the reader and the writer. When that negative self-talk kicks up, remember to translate the harsh words into the language of the kind critic:

This matters to you.

You care.

You care about the impact of your writing.

You are sensitive, thoughtful, and creative.

You are having an experience.

Your voice matters. Keep going.

Chapter Twenty-One Activities

In the Zone

🕐 40 minutes

When do you feel in the zone? Explore your feelings about the different Story Cycles.

Step 1: Use list making to reflect on the Story Cycles.

> For each cycle, write a love-hate list. This is like a pro-con list, but the focus is on what you like vs. what you don't like, what's comfortable vs. uncomfortable, difficult vs. easy.

- ◎ Calibrate Cycle . . .
- 🪷 Cultivate Cycle . . .
- 🌅 Collaborate Cycle . . .
- ⛰ Craft Cycle . . .

Step 2: Review your lists and assess how you feel about each Story Cycle.
- Which cycles are comfortable?
- Which cycles are uncomfortable?

Step 3: Use freewriting to uncover the fear that might be driving aversion.

> Prompt: The [X Cycle] is scary because . . .

Once you know your comfort zone, use this information to triage a situation.

_____

_____

_____

_____

_____

Pack your backpack

45 minutes

What discoveries did you make? What will you pack for the journey ahead? Use your Field Notes Writing Tracker to reflect and write. Use freewriting and list making to explore these questions.

- ☐ What are three things you learned?
- ☐ What are three favorite exercises?
- ☐ What is your biggest challenge at the moment?
- ☐ What are new insights about your process? About the craft? What writing routines worked and didn't work for you?
- ☐ What are good places to write? Time of day? Special treats?
- ☐ Any new rituals or routines?
- ☐ How has your framework for process changed?
- ☐ What measurable markers are effective or ineffective? Consider pages, words, time, a specific element.
- ☐ What have you discovered about your story?

_____

_____

_____

_____

_____

_____

_____

_____

_____

Take Two

⏰ 40 minutes

☐ Repeat the Story Cycle survey (Chapter Four)

- What is your current project?

- What's the status of the project?

- Talk about your process.

- What is your intended outcome?

- What would you like to accomplish?

☐ Now look back at the initial Calibrate Your Compass answers from Chapter One.

- How do your answers compare?

- How has your project evolved?

☐ Did you take a different direction?

- If it has changed, how so?

- How do you feel about this?

☐ What discoveries have you made?

☐ What questions have come to the surface?

☐ Did your initial assessment match the reality?

- If not, how was it different?

☐ What was the intended outcome?

- If you achieved this outcome, does it feel the way you expected?

_____

_____

_____

_____

_____

_____

About the Author

Sascha Brown Rice is an award-winning filmmaker, writer, coach, and teacher. Her Emmy-nominated documentary *California State of Mind* and her feature rom-com *Mango Kiss* both won multiple honors, screened internationally, and were broadcast (on Netflix, public television, Logo, and more). Producing projects include the feature film *Solace*, the web series *Black Kungfu Chick*, and the short film *Basurero*. In her role as consulting producer for the Central Valley's Big Tell, Rice has mentored dozens of filmmakers and shepherded over seventy short docs to completion. As the Global Marketing Director for Eastman Kodak's motion picture division, she amplified Kodak's visibility with innovative collaborations, strategic partnerships, and community engagement. Rice  supported marketing initiatives for an array of projects including commercials, music videos, fine art museum pieces, and notable television and feature films: blockbusters like *Star Wars: The Force Awakens*, and *Batman v Superman*; hit shows like AMC's *The Walking Dead*; indie favorites like *The Hateful Eight* and *Carol*; and Academy Award-winners like *La La Land*.

Rice is driven by a passion for making art and making a difference. As the granddaughter of California's former Governor Pat Brown, niece of four-term Governor Jerry Brown, and daughter of former State Treasurer Kathleen Brown, Rice is committed to carrying on her family legacy of civic engagement and serves on the Board of Advisors of the Pat Brown Institute, which is a nonpartisan public policy Institute at Cal State LA. Other notable projects have included The Audience Awards' Women's Film Challenge and R.O.W. (RIVER OF WINGS), a public art installation of interactive kinetic sculptures aimed to bring awareness to LA River revitalization via giant bird sculptures personalized and reimagined by local schools, community groups, and artists.

With over twenty-five years in the industry, Rice offers clients a wealth of practical, strategic, and creative insights. She mentors both experienced writers who seek to rekindle their creative fire and emerging storytellers just beginning their writing journey.

Additional Publications by Sascha Brown Rice

The Story Cycle Method: A Practical Playbook for Writers and Dreamers

The Companion Journals:
  The Compass Notebook: A Story Cycle Guided Journal
  The Field Notes Writing Tracker: A Story Cycle Process Journal

Making is
messy.

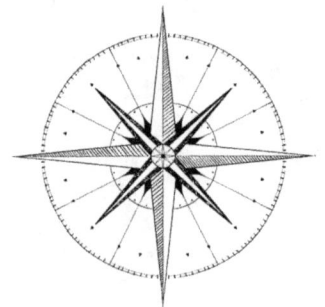

www.ingramcontent.com/pod-product-compliance
Lightning Source LLC
Chambersburg PA
CBHW082144120626
46553CB00010B/2759